To Betty,
The best conversations
start with 2 words...
"Remember when..."
Enjoy,
7/26/16

Tricks, Horses, and Rock and Roll

Tricks, Horses, and Rock and Roll

by
Robb W. MacDonald

TWO HARBORS PRESS

Copyright © 2011 by Robb W. MacDonald.

Two Harbors Press
212 3ʳᵈ Avenue North, Suite 290
Minneapolis, MN 55401
612.455.2293
www.TwoHarborsPress.com

All rights reserved. No part of this publication may be reproduced, stored in a retrieval system, or transmitted, in any form or by any means, electronic, mechanical, photocopying, recording, or otherwise, without the prior written permission of the author.

ISBN-13: 978-1-937293-20-8
LCCN: 2011935201

Distributed by Itasca Books

Cover Design by Elsa Angvall
Typeset by Steve Porter

Printed in the United States of America

DEDICATION

This book is dedicated to my dear departed grandpa, Boyd Oliver Wallace. It was he who instilled in me the ability to, as my mother puts it, "make a good story better."

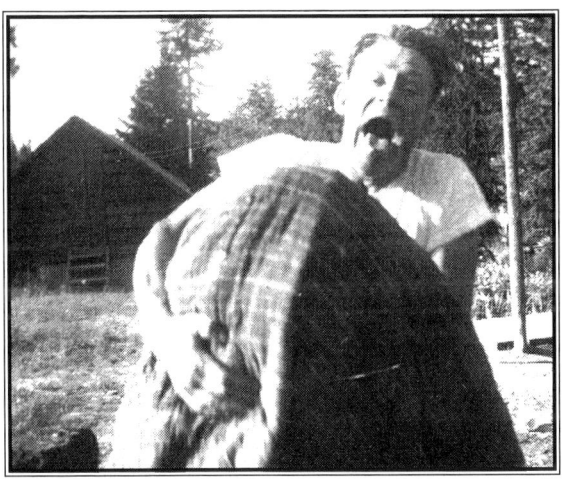

My Grandpa (and Grandma under blanket) Wallace

FOREWORD AND ACKNOWLEDGEMENTS

Welcome to *Tricks, Horses, and Rock and Roll*. The whole purpose of putting these stories together is to try to spark the readers' own memories of times gone by. I have no misgivings that some folks who grew up in big cities, or even in vastly different areas of our great country, may not relate to some of the material presented. I do believe, however, that all of us, regardless of where or when we were kids, have some very vivid memories of happy, simple things that seem to get harder and harder to come by with advancing years. I can't count how many times I have been stopped by someone who has read some of these stories and been told, "I loved this story or that because it reminded me of a time when my brother and I . . ." I love that, as I am a firm believer that what is truly important in our lives is the memories we make.

As you will read, I was born in a small town in the northernmost tip of the great state of Idaho. I lived on a small ranch, with what would now be deemed a "conventional" family. My elder brother of two years, Rowdy, and I were blessed to have horses, room, and parents who loved us enough to set us free. Granted, it was a different time than today when you could let your kids go out riding or playing from dawn till dark without worry that they would be all right.

I began writing these stories in 1998. Originally they were meant for my extended family only. I wrote them out with pen and paper in moments stolen from my true profession, a tire guy, and handed them out around Christmas. Obviously, my family loved them. This didn't come as a great shock to me, as they were my family—what were they going to say? However, a funny thing happened. My family started giving out my stories to friends and neighbors, and they loved them, as well. Still, I thought, most of them knew me, or knew of me, so again, what were they going to say? My darling wife of thirty years, Jeannie, who for some unexplainable reason has always believed in me, started after me to put these stories into book form so that everyone could see them. Since my formal education ended after graduating high school, it seemed evident to me that I was nowhere near smart enough to write a book. I got a D- in typing, for crying out loud! Enter two wonderful sisters-in-law, Summer and Judy. Both of them volunteered to type up my stories, and Summer formatted them into little booklets for a local craft fair. Much to my amazement, she sold every one.

I've continued writing, and with copious encouragement from the love of my life, I have finally gotten up the courage to put what I consider some of my favorite stories together in *Tricks, Horses, and Rock and Roll*. I hope you will enjoy reading it even half as much as I did writing it.

INTRODUCTION

When I was first introduced to the stories in *Tricks, Horses, and Rock and Roll*, I was transported back in time to a simple era that reminded me of my own childhood in rural southern Idaho. These stories, with their vivid detail and homey dialogue, sparked memories that I hadn't been in touch with for far too long. Since the author and I share a love for northern Idaho (I've lived in Idaho all my life but moved from the extreme southern part of the state to the extreme northern part fifteen years ago), and all things real, it only stood to reason that I would thoroughly enjoy this book. I encourage you to find a quiet spot, kick up your feet, and take your own trip down memory lane with *Tricks, Horses, and Rock and Roll*.

Wags,
Dr. Marty Becker, "America's Veterinarian"

CONTENTS

DEDICATION v
FOREWORD AND ACKNOWLEDGEMENTS vii
INTRODUCTION ix
Chapter 1 – . . . FOR DISTANCE 1
Chapter 2 – THE TRUTH ABOUT GREAT IDEAS 5
Chapter 3 – THE GREAT MAC BARN RODEO 11
Chapter 4 – BRAIN ROT (And Other TV Side Effects) 15
Chapter 5 – BARREL DOGGIN' 23
Chapter 6 – TRICKS, HORSES, AND ROCK AND ROLL 29
Chapter 7 – TO DINE OR KNOTS 33
Chapter 8 – TALKIN' COWBOY 39
Chapter 9 – BAZOOKA MADNESS 43
Chapter 10 – TAKING FLIGHT 51
Chapter 11 – CALF RIDIN' 55
Chapter 12 – PRINTETH AND FRECKLES 59
Chapter 13 – RODEO SCOUTS 65
Chapter 14 – NAME GAME 79
Chapter 15 – 4-H CAMP 83
Chapter 16 – HORSE WRECKS 93
Chapter 17 – PRINCIPLE MATTERS 101
Chapter 18 – SLEDDING DOS AND DON'TS 107
Chapter 19 – BEAR SLAYER 113
Chapter 20 – BACKPACKING DONE RIGHT 121
Chapter 21 – CRICK FISHIN' 127
Chapter 22 – FUN WITH EXPLOSIVES 133
Chapter 23 – A HARROWING EXPERIENCE 141
Chapter 24 – IT'S A CRASH TEST, DUMMY 149
Chapter 25 – HI HO SILVER! 155
Chapter 26 – THE GATES OF HELL 163
ABOUT THE AUTHOR 169
PHOTO CREDITS 170

Chapter 1

... FOR DISTANCE

I was born a cowboy. From the top of my bulbous head to the tips of my sloped middle toes, I was made for life aboard a horse. And so it was as far back as I remember.

My first horse was moody; that also happened to be his name. He gave me wings to fly on my own and more than once the proper motivation to do so. He was a grand steed and a credit to the Shetland pony breed. My mom got Moody from my Grandpa Wallace in a controversial trade for a brand new saddle that was given to her by Dad. Turns out it was a trade of a lifetime. It was widely believed the deal was arranged so my big brother, Rowdy, could have a horse of his own. This was always accepted, since for the first two or three years Moody was a member of our family I hardly ever got to ride him. But when the time came that I thought I had enough large motor skills to stay aloft, he was mine. I think I was three years old. Since I had finally grown into my horse, this sadly left Rowdy without.

That malady was short lived, however, when Ginger

stepped gracefully into the picture. She was a striking beauty, with her dark gray coat and brilliant white mane. She possessed a fire like none we had ever known. Where Moody was the proverbial tortoise, Ginger was the elusive hare. Rowdy found out many times just how elusive she could be. We all said Ginger was Rowdy's horse but, alas, I'm sure we were all very aware that she belonged to no one. Granted, most of the time she played along, but when push came to shove, it was no contest. So there we were: Rowdy, Robb, Moody, and Ginger, a quartet for the ages, indivisible and, more importantly, fully mobile. This mobility afforded us a world unreachable to most kids, or adults for that matter. On any spring morning we could be seen chasing imaginary rustlers or horse thieves off our place, and by afternoon we would be up in the woods discovering lost lands and loot long abandoned by bank robbers and renegade Indians.

We were always shocked at how careless those bad guys must have been to leave some of the treasure behind in their haste to escape our wrath. Stuff like perfectly good doorknobs, jar lids, car headlights, and even a genuine pocketknife, complete with a pre-broken blade.

Sometimes we weren't allowed to collect the spoils of our adventures, as Ginger seemed to have a very distinct concept of good and evil. If she didn't like it, you left it—or she left you, as simple as that. Moody was far more tolerant and would allow almost anything to be hoisted across his broad shoulders, and I'm sure this disgusted poor Ginger to death. I loved him for that.

As time passed, we constantly searched for new, more exciting things to do on our outings. Trick riding, for instance, seemed like a logical choice. Logical, that is, until you try it.

Our first attempt was probably that of the Simple Stand. This trick was, of course, one of our first attempts, and it was just as it sounds: simply a matter of standing on your horse's bare back while it stood munching on grass. We became bored with this very quickly and set about discovering new, more difficult and dangerous tricks. Turns out, Ginger was a big help in this endeavor, as she also became bored with simply standing in one place. Hence, the birth of the Moving Stand Trick, which consisted of standing on your horse's back while it was moving. This maneuver wasn't bad bareback, but with a saddle . . . it's a wonder that Rowdy and I ever had kids. Eventually we both became quite adept at these two tricks, and aside from the occasional mishap, which usually involved Ginger sending Rowdy careening into the pucker brush, we reached the point where it was nothing unusual for us to be seen loping through the forest standing atop our sturdy ponies.

One hot summer day as we lounged in the shade of a large Ponderosa Pine tree, laying flat on Moody's broad back, utilizing his ample rump as a pillow, I felt a calling. It was nature, and I instantly regretted the consumption of the Orange Crush I had packed in my nap sack for lunch. Since I was only five at the time, and stood all of three feet four in height, dismounting my steed to heed nature's call was somewhat of a bother. After dismounting, I had to search for a suitable stump or rock to climb up onto in order to achieve enough elevation to mount back up. Taking a quick look around, I saw no such suitable perches nearby. Since this was the case, I decided to do what seemed perfectly natural at the time. I stood atop Moody's back and, as they say, let 'er rip. Since Moody was preoccupied with some delicious treat, he was not bothered in the slightest by the stream cascading off his back to the ground below.

"Hey, cool!" Rowdy said, as he recognized a new trick when he saw it.

"I wonder if Ginger would go for that?" he asked, more

to himself than to me.

Having finished, I plopped back down on Moody's back, very satisfied with myself having impressed my big brother.

Rowdy, never one to be out done, leapt up on Ginger's back to try to duplicate the feat. As I mentioned before, Ginger seemed to have a very strong feeling about what was good and what was evil. This, it seemed, struck her as extremely evil. Since it was her station in life to stamp out all things evil, Rowdy had scarcely begun to relieve himself when Ginger snapped her head up and took off.

"Whoa!" Rowdy screamed as Ginger's walk became a trot. I sat on Moody, both confused and amused by the predicament Rowdy now found himself in. I must say he showed amazing dexterity in his effort to stay aboard his misbehaving mount for as long as he did. Eventually though, his inability to sit down, coupled with his lack of ability to balance himself with his hands, was more than he could overcome. Off into the pucker brush he flew, all the while spewing a steady stream of seven-year-old profanities, among other things, on his way. Slowly Moody and I moved forward to the place in the brush where all matter of commotion was taking place and waited patiently for Rowdy to emerge. Over the sound of my raucous laughter, I heard the distinct sound of a zipper and saw the brush parting as Rowdy made his way back to the trail.

So was born the incredible Bareback Stand Up and Whiz for Distance Trick. As it turned out, this trick is so rare and dynamic that I've never to this day seen it repeated. It's very risky, as one false move by man or horse could mean tragedy, as my big brother found out that first day.

Chapter 2

THE TRUTH ABOUT GREAT IDEAS

When I was a boy, there were three things that I knew without a shadow of a doubt were the gospel truth. First was that gunsels were detestable; second was that Bazooka was manna sent down from the heavens; and third was that any idea my brother came up with, no matter how bizarre, was a great one. This third truth was tested by fire more than once, even literally on some occasions—like the time he convinced me that it was a *great idea* to throw an empty aerosol can into the burn barrel. I lost all my eyebrows in the resultant fireball and am sure that if I'd had any hair on my head, I'd have lost that, as well. Still it was exciting and thus proved to be just another *great idea*.

It is said that idle hands are the devil's workshop. This may be true, but I always found that idle hands were also very conducive to Rowdy's *great ideas*. If in fact necessity is the mother of invention, then boredom is the grandmother.

I'll never forget one day when sheer boredom necessitated the mother of all inventions, one of Rowdy's *greatest ideas*. The year was 1967; I was five years old. Rowdy was seven and well on his way to fulfilling his destiny as a creative genius. It was a gray, rainy day outside, and it seems that by noon we had exhausted our reserve of rainy day projects. By this stage of our young lives, we were already well aware of the consequences of bemoaning our lack of something to do to our mother, as she was always ready and willing to *find* something to keep us busy. These things she would find were always something far less than desirable. Things like cleaning our room, organizing our toy box, digging ditches then filling them in, et cetera, et cetera. Mom, it seemed, was not the direct link to my brother's *great idea* gene.

As we moped around the house, our small heads wagging from side to side, eyes glazed over firmly in the clutches of boredom, Rowdy caught a glimpse of my mother looking at us with the unmistakable look of someone *finding* something for us to do.

"Quick! To the basement," Rowdy whispered, giving me a helpful shove toward the door that led downstairs. I complied with his request, as I knew by casting a quick look in my mother's direction why he was in such a hurry to get out of sight.

"We're going down to the basement!" Rowdy shouted over his shoulder as we scurried out the door, closing it behind us. As we headed down the narrow stairway, I was grateful for my big brother's alertness, knowing that his quick thinking had in all likelihood saved us from a fate worse than death. I also hoped that the change in environment might spark one of his *great ideas*. I wasn't disappointed. As we reached the bottom of the stairs and flipped on the light, it seemed Rowdy's *great idea* mechanism clicked on, as well.

"Hey," he said, "would you look at that?"

"What?" I asked, seeing nothing but a cardboard box sitting in the middle of the floor. It seems where I saw a box,

Rowdy saw an Indy Car, and he wasted no time jumping into the driver's seat.

"Hop in," he said. "Let's take this baby for a spin."

I did as I was told and quickly joined in making our best and loudest car noises. We leaned left, leaned right, grabbing gear after gear as we screamed around our imaginary racetrack. We rolled once or twice, as I recall, and once even wheelied our cardboard chariot over backwards. It was great fun for awhile. Sadly, after approximately five hundred laps, the tipping back and forth and making car noises lost some of its pizzazz. Once again, we found ourselves slipping into the dark envelope of boredom. Fortunately, Rowdy's *great idea* supply was abundant.

"Let's make a real car out of this thing," he said, and we set about fixing up our boxcar. We took some crayons and fashioned some dazzling racing stripes, some old coffee can lids were fitted as headlights, and I was able to find an old tricycle wheel that made a perfect steering wheel.

As we stepped back and admired our creation, congratulating each other on our resourcefulness, it dawned on us that we couldn't waste such a masterpiece of ingenuity. We had to drive this "Bad Boy," but where? The answer to that question wasn't long coming.

"We need a hill!" I said. "Or something."

"Or something," Rowdy mused, and I could tell he was exploring options as he had assumed his *deep thought posture*. This posture involved placing his right elbow in the palm of his left hand while stroking his chin with the fingers of his right hand. Normally he'd also make some deep thought noises such as, "Hmmm, hmmm." Invariably this posture brought results, and this time was no exception. I saw the light come on as I stared into his wide, brown eyes.

"I've got a *great idea*!" he proclaimed. "We'll take it down the stairs!"

"How did he do that?" I wondered as I watched him latch on to the box/car and head for the stairway. As I followed, watching the box bounce up the steps behind him, I marveled at my big brother's wisdom. Why hadn't I thought of taking the car down the stairs? It seemed so obvious now. We needed a hill; well, heck; we had one built right into our own house. When we reached the landing at the top of the stairs, we situated our car at the starting point and surveyed what lay before us. The course was pretty simple: twelve steps down to a landing, then a sharp right turn into the basement.

Standing at the top looking down, it occurred to me that I had never really realized just how steep our stairway was. I mentioned this fact to Rowdy, who assured me that it just looked that way because of poor lighting and the fact that the concrete wall at the bottom hindered my depth perception. "Of course," I thought to myself, "how could I be so foolish?"

I hopped into the backseat and prepared myself for the exciting trip to come. Rowdy, however, didn't immediately take his position in the driver's seat, but instead stood looking first down the stairs, then at the car. Down the stairs, then back at the car again. Since he had once again assumed his *deep thought posture*, I sat silently watching him tap his fingertips on his chin.

"I think," he said finally, "that after figuring the degree of downward slope, added together with the probable speed, combined with the proximity of the concrete wall at the bottom of the stairs, that maybe it would be best if *you* sat up front and drove the car this first trip."

He went on to explain that because of his weight being much greater than mine, he was needed in the rear to prevent us from being over weighted in the nose and possibly adversely affecting the handling of our car.

I was, of course, overwhelmed. What a great and wise brother I had—and so kind to let me drive. I slid forward into the driver's seat and pulled my imaginary goggles down over my eyes. As Rowdy crawled in behind me, I took the wheel and started making my best Indy Car noises. Spit droplets cascaded down the stairway before me as I revved my engine, awaiting the green light.

"Ready . . . Set . . . Gooo!" Rowdy shouted as he and I lurched forward, sending our box, I mean car, over the edge. We picked up speed rapidly, more rapidly in fact than I believe either of us could have imagined. As we neared the midway point, our speed reaching approximately eighty miles per hour, I leaned left and turned the wheel, trying to better position us for the hairpin turn I knew we had to make at the bottom. Much to my dismay, there was no response. I turned and turned again and still no response. Now I was getting somewhat concerned. I tried the brake and realized that this was an area we had somehow overlooked. I cursed myself for my short sightedness as the concrete wall raced up to meet us.

"LEAN!!!!" Rowdy screamed as we neared the bottom. We both leaned hard right, hoping to somehow steer the runaway vehicle away from the wall looming directly before us. The boxcar tipped to the right, then smashed into the wall. Fortunately for Rowdy, he was able to utilize my small, yet somewhat soft, body as a sort of human airbag, and he was spared serious injury. I, on the other hand, gained a lifelong respect for airbags.

I'm not able to remember much about the crash, itself, as it seems I was involved watching a short movie featuring the life and times of a small boy who much resembled myself flashing before my eyes. There is one thought that I can remember having, however, as my body made contact with concrete that day. I realized there were now two things that I knew without a shadow of a doubt were the gospel truth. One of those involved gunsels, the other Bazooka Bubble Gum.

Chapter 3

THE GREAT MAC BARN RODEO

During all of my young life, my dad was a rodeo cowboy. I have little doubt that this simple hobby had more to do with the way I've turned out than anything else I can imagine.

For the better part of ten years, my brothers and I were cowboy kids. Hat to boot tip, dyed-in-the-wool redneck, straw-sucking, Bazooka-chewing cowboy kids. It was grand times.

My little brother, Ron (yes, Ronald MacDonald), was around for only about the last four years of that period. I often wished it had been longer, but things change.

Being cowboys meant horses and rodeos to Rowdy, and me. Since we had horses, in the forms of Moody and Ginger, a rodeo was only a few strides and an old corn stalk away.

One day as we languished about fighting a losing battle with boredom, Rowdy was struck with one of his much loved and anticipated *great ideas*. It went something like this: We would get Dad's old bareback riggin' and cinch up my old pony, Moody. We would make a buckin' flank out of twine and use an old dried out corn stalk for a "hot shot," or prod. It was to be the greatest rodeo ever known to man. I will note here that backyard rodeos were forbidden. I can to this day recite the variety of reasons that backyard rodeos were forbidden, and I can assure you they all probably made sense. However, as with many forbidden activities, the potential for fun (our most sought after commodity) often outweighed reason. This is not to say that we were willing to disregard our parents' wishes just willy-nilly. We obviously were sure to take the proper precautions. A quick scan from the hayloft confirmed that Dad was at work, Mom was occupied, and all systems were go. We bailed out of the loft and snapped up a couple cans of grain to gather the stock, which I'm sure knew something was amiss all along. They approached cautiously. Since Moody was part pig, he managed to push his way under and around the big horses and deposited his nose in my can. I snapped the lead rope to his halter, and the show was on. Miraculously, Ginger was also caught and tethered for the second go around. She wasn't tickled one bit about it either. I'm sure I have mentioned about Ginger's strong sense of good and evil; unfortunately for us, this seemed to strike her as evil.

We outfitted Moody with the old riggin', which was not much more than a leather suitcase handle tied to a ten- to twelve-inch piece of thick leather, and went to the feeder in the lean-to that served as our chute.

I crawled aboard, pulled down my hat, and nodded for the imaginary gate. Rowdy pulled up the flank as he jabbed my bronc in the belly with the corn stalk. Near as I can remember, I got four good crow hops in before I bit the dust. The rodeo was a success.

As I got up and dusted myself off, Rowdy shot back into the barn for another love offering of grain, and Moody was soon back into the lean-to area. Rowdy's turn was nowhere near as spectacular, as Moody decided he didn't want to play this silly game and just trotted around the corral. It was bumpy, but it wasn't bucking, and Rowdy felt gypped. Since Ginger was fresh, it seemed perfectly natural that she would be the feature of the Great Mac Barn Rodeo.

We started cinching her up, and she swelled up like a balloon. We waited patiently till she had to let out some air and tightened up the gear. As we led her into the lean-to, she stalked like an upset teenager and tried (successfully, I might add) to give the impression that little boys can get hurt playing rodeo at home.

Technically, it was my turn to ride, but since I felt so guilty about my horse's poor performance for Rowdy, I granted him a re-ride. I assure you that this had nothing whatsoever to do with the fact that I had absolutely no desire to mess with Ginger. I held the agitated bronc as Rowdy mounted up and went through the ritual face slapping and deep breathing. He pulled his hat over his eyes and ears and nodded. What happened next is still sort of blurry, as I saw most of it from my back. I dropped the lead line and jerked the flank twine without much reaction, but then I touched her stomach with the broken corn stalk. The eruption that followed paled that of Mount Saint Helens. With a look of utter disgust and unabated hatred, Ginger wheeled around and planted the side of her sizable cheek next to mine. I was promptly launched across the lean-to, and as I landed softly in a conveniently placed pile of straw and horse leavings, I watched in amazement and horror as the ride took shape.

Ginger took two small jumps, which I thought Rowdy handled quite well. Then everything faded to slow motion, and time nearly stood still. The third jump was high, probably twelve feet straight up, or so it seemed. At the apex of this monumental leap, Ginger turned over on her side, executing the most perfect sunfish maneuver I have ever seen. Needless to say, when she came back to the upright position, her rider was shoulder deep in dust. Rowdy stood there on his head for several minutes, then fell over, presumably dead. I made my way out of my pile, brushing the hay and other material from my clothes, all the while trying to get the horsehair spit out of my mouth. Rowdy started coming around and rolled to look at me. His face was covered with dirt. A little piece of horse apple hung from his scraped and bleeding chin. He grinned sickly and shook his head. He gave all appearances of being a survivor, so I started to laugh uncontrollably. Ah yes, I thought, the Great Mac Barn Rodeo was a tremendous success.

Chapter 4

BRAIN ROT
(And Other TV Side Effects)

As I reflect back on my early years, it occurs to me that the relatively small amount of television that I was exposed to, in some ways, had a profound effect on my life.

I say that I was exposed to a relatively small amount of TV. This in comparison to people of my day, not to people of today, as I'm sure that my kids watch more TV in a week than my brother and I did from 1965 through 1977.

My parents ruled the TV and demanded a very hands-off approach. Except for Saturday morning, Rowdy and I were not to touch approach or even gaze upon our nineteen-inch black and white screen without the express written consent of Mom and Dad or the National Television Board of America. Defiance or wanton disregard of this or any other rule set down by the aforementioned resulted in the most severe punishment allowed by the laws of the State of Idaho. Such punishment included, but was not limited to, being hung by one's thumbs from the nearest clothesline, having one's ears boxed, or the ever-popular skinning one alive. Needless to say, Rowdy and I were always in most strict compliance with these rules.

During the week the TV was never turned on till at least six p.m. That was when the news was on and served as Rowdy's and my signal to leave the room as quickly as possible, lest we risk a slow and horrific death from boredom. Usually we would flee to the basement or out to the barn where we could almost always find some kind of mischief to get into. News time was always an excellent time for mischief, as Mom and Dad were so utterly enthralled with the news of the day that they noticed very little else. This came in handy from time to time as all boys, I'm convinced; require a certain amount of mischief to grow into well-rounded adults. As I look at doctors, lawyers, and other such maladjusted men, it occurs to me that most of them must have lacked sufficient mischief as kids.

After the evening news, and whatever destructive deed we had taken on for the night, Rowdy and I would make our way to our appointed spots in front of the tube, that being a prone position, chins propped in hands, roughly four feet from the glowing screen. There we would stay, except for bathroom breaks or snack emergencies, until bedtime or eight thirty p.m.

Saturdays, however, were another story altogether. On Saturday, or Cartoon Day as it was referred to at our house, we kids were able to throw most of the week's stringent rules out the window. Cartoon Day was our day, and as such we were allowed to gaze upon, approach, and, yes, even touch the TV from the time we got up, roughly six thirty a.m., till cartoons were over around noon, without fear of reprisal.

It was on a Saturday such as this when Rowdy and I got a hard lesson in the destructive nature of television and its influence. It was a day I'll never forget.

It started out as a normal Cartoon Day, that day in 1967,

with Rowdy and me on the couch watching Bugs, Daffy, and the gang. Mom and Dad were getting ready to go somewhere that afternoon, and since it was rainy and miserable, we had been given the okay to watch TV after the normal shut off time of noon. This was exciting for us, as it gave us an opportunity to watch *Championship Wrestling,* brought to us by the friendly folks at Dr. David Cowan's Peerless Dentist, located in the Paulsen Building in beautiful downtown Spokane.

We were very thankful to Dr. Cowan, as without him and his *Championship Wrestling,* Rowdy and I would probably have grown up to be nothing more than sniveling wimps, groveling in the face of adversity. As it was, however, we were thankfully exposed to such heroes as The Giant, The Masked Mauler, and, of course, The Claw, with his famed sleeper hold.

The Claw was an incredible man, and by simply gripping his opponents in such a way as to put pressure on their temples with his tremendous thumb and fingers, he was able to put them into a sound sleep, affording him an easy pin. The Claw was always my personal favorite.

As Mom and Dad left the house that day, Mom recited the ever-present warnings, such as don't make a mess and don't get soaked and catch "ammonia." They could not know of the bizarre events to come.

As soon as we heard the truck leave the driveway, Rowdy and I sprinted back to our bedroom and grabbed our faithful teddy bears, Reuben and Pinky. They were always used when our parents weren't around. They were used, of course, as our personal wrestling opponents and did an admirable job of it. Old Reuben could take a Flying Mare from the arm of a sofa, an elbow to the ribs, and even . . . yes, even my version of The Claw without so much as batting an eye. He did actually suffer a broken eye button once, but that was the result of a nightmarish Helicopter Spin into the refrigerator handle. He was a tough, tough little bear.

On that day, as Rowdy and I tossed, kicked, and clawed our bears, I began to get hot. Hot and dry. It was time for a drink. I dropped my now submissive opponent and strolled over to the fridge to inspect the menu of the day. As I swung the door open and took a brief inventory of the beverages available, my five-year-old eyes settled upon what seemed to me to be the answer to my parched throat. It was a lone bottle of Olympia Beer. The neat looking little round bottle seemed to beckon to me as I stood basking in the coolness emanating from the refrigerator. I should say, as I closed my small hand around the neck of the cool, brown bottle, that it did occur to me that beer was probably not the drink of choice recommended by nine out of ten moms of five-year-old boys. I gave that some thought as I closed the refrigerator door and began searching for a bottle opener. As I was scouring the drawers, Rowdy apparently heard the commotion in the kitchen and rightly suspected that I may be up to no good. He popped his head around the corner, still dangling Pinky by one ear, and obviously couldn't believe his eyes. I say obviously because his eyes instantly became the size of Pinky's, which were enormous.

"What the heck do you think you're doing, mister man?" Rowdy asked in his most stern seven-year-old voice.

I, being just a little surprised by his apparent conservatism, answered as honestly and plainly as I could.

"I'm thirsty, and I'm havin' a beer," I said, continuing to search for a bottle opener.

"No you're not!" Rowdy blurted in utter disbelief.

Now normally, Rowdy and I got along marvelously. He was, of course, "the all-knowing, all-seeing one," and usually whatever he said was good for me. For that simple reason I was known to much of my family as "Me Too" for years. But on this day, I felt different. I felt independent. I felt confident. And after watching forty-five minutes of wrestling and beating my teddy to pulp, I felt *tough*.

I was, however, at a loss for a witty comeback to Rowdy's, "No you're not!" comment, so I did the next best thing. I simply ignored him. Rowdy didn't take kindly to my insolence, and I'm sure the responsibility for my well being weighed heavily on his young psyche. That, I feel, is what probably led him to his next course of action. That being a tight headlock and a stream of seven-year-old profanities.

"Put down that ---- beer you little ----!" he seethed through clenched teeth.

I didn't particularly care for his methods, and so I set about trying to remove my head from his lock.

"No!" I shouted. "It's my beer, and I'm gonna have it!"

We wrestled around on the kitchen floor, scrapping and calling each other names until something dawned on me that I'd seen in a western movie. I'd simply break the bottle over his overbearing head. Even if it cost me the seemingly precious contents, it would be worth it to one, get him off me, and two, finally after all these years show Mr. Big Shot who was boss. I gripped the stubby neck of the bottle and swung it backward over my shoulder just where I knew his head would be and braced myself for the crash that was to come.

Unfortunately, the sound that came from that point was something less than I'd anticipated. Instead of a dramatic crash, like in the movies, it was more of a less dramatic clunk, followed by an enraged growl. The next sound to reach my ears was a series of clunks that were the result of my hard little head making contact with the equally hard linoleum floor.

Realizing that I was facing imminent death, and that dying with a beer bottle firmly clutched in my hand was probably not my direct ticket to heaven, I dropped the bottle and concentrated on every championship wrestling move I'd ever seen. I tried the Back Bridge, the Twisting Hip Toss, and, yes, even The Claw, all to no avail. Clunk, clunk, clunk went my head as Rowdy clung to my ears and continued banging my head on the floor, spewing profanities all the while. Fortunately for me, I was blessed with a cast iron head, so I didn't sustain any permanent damage.

Since I had tried every move I could think of with no success, I decided it was high time to do what I did best. Cheat. I waited for Rowdy to raise my head one more time, and I wrenched my entire body to the left, grabbing his right forearm and firmly planting my teeth into the flesh on it. With a scream he momentarily released his grip, and I was able to bridge him off of my chest. I rolled out from under him, and like a shot from a gun, made my hasty retreat to the bathroom, locking the door behind me.

As I recall, I stayed there for what seemed an hour or so, hoping that eventually Rowdy would cool off enough to let me go on living. When I finally came out and peeked around the corner, I found Rowdy sitting on the couch, rubbing the red mark on his arm.

I walked over and jumped up on the couch beside him.

"Sorry for bitin' ya," I said, genuinely sorry that I had stooped so low.

"Stupid," he said, not altogether unaffectionately. Then he just sat there staring at the TV.

I felt awful. "What had possessed me?" I wondered. Then I realized it had to be the TV and *Championship Wrestling*. I remembered that Mom had always told us that too much TV would rot our brains. I turned to Rowdy to tell him what I thought and noticed the growing goose egg on his forehead.

"Sorry 'bout hittin' ya with the bottle," I said.

"Stupid," he replied.

"Wanna turn off the boob tube and go bike ridin' in the

rain and catch ammonia?" I asked, desperately trying to break the tension.

"Sure," he said, rubbing his forehead, "stupid."

As we went riding in the rain, I found myself reflecting on the events of the day. Had my brain actually rotted like Mom had said it would? Was there some subliminal message telling me that I needed a beer? Or was I just being what Rowdy had said, stupid?

"If that's what Rowdy thinks," I thought to myself, "I guess me, too."

Chapter 5

BARREL DOGGIN'

From the time I was born till I was around fourteen years old, my brother and I spent every weekend of summer at one rodeo or another, chasing the circuit with my father. Since we were too young to compete in the "real McCoy," we were compelled to improvise. We did so by creating our very own home rodeos.

To create a home rodeo, the only ingredients required are two eager young cowboys, a working dad, an occupied mom, and two Shetland ponies. Mix the two young cowboys together with ponies; add three parts danger, one part creativity, a pinch of busy parents; and store in a large corral for four to five hours.

The result of your concoction may turn out many different ways. It could be entertaining, scary, or extremely painful and nerve racking. Ours were always great. I have to say we whipped up a darn fine home rodeo. Some of the events included barrel racing, pole bending, post roping, and finally barrel doggin'. Barrel racing, we knew, was normally reserved as a lady's event in regular rodeo, but since we were always firm believers in gender equality, not to mention our limited resources, we gladly ran the cloverleaf pattern. Rowdy and his pony, Ginger, always burned through the course like pros. Ginger, you see, was the fastest pony in three counties. Rowdy was extremely proud of this fact, and he was always more than happy to prove it. Moody and I completed the course, also, but I believe our efforts were more of a smolder than an actual burn. Nevertheless, I can proudly say that we never knocked over a single barrel and, therefore, avoided any five-second penalties. Still, it never was our best event. I should note here that my pony, Moody, was what could only be referred to as "speed challenged," or perhaps "velocity deficient." He was, I'm convinced, the greatest Shetland pony to ever walk the face of the earth; it's just that he did so *very* slowly.

Pole bending was always the second event in our home rodeos. Although pole bending was never a real rodeo event, since we had poles, it was a natural. This event is not well known, but is the horse version of slalom. You simply weave your mount through a series of poles, once up, once back, and then sprint to the finish.

Rowdy and Ginger zipped through the course, breaking home rodeo world records. Moody and I also completed the course. We could well have turned in a few records in this event, although they probably would appear at the opposite end of the page from Rowdy and Ginger's.

Moody's and my lack of dominance in the first two events didn't cause us much concern, as we both knew our best events were yet to come. You see, in these events we held the advantages.

Post roping, for instance, was an event that required timing, not necessarily flat out speed, and this is where Moody and I specialized. Granted, post roping is a timed event, and a certain amount of speed is required, but it can be your downfall, as Rowdy and Ginger never seemed to learn.

Post roping was once again not recognized as real rodeo event, but it was our own invention and always proved to be very exciting and entertaining. Post roping was patterned after calf roping, but since we lacked a supply of calves, and had an almost infinite supply of fence posts, we made due. The event went like this: The roper lined up directly across the corral from the designated roping post; he and his horse then sprinted across the corral, roped the post, rapidly dismounted, ran to the fence, climbed it, and wrapped his rope three times around the top of the post. Less than three wraps got you a five-second penalty, as the fence would surely have kicked free.

Most days our event went something like this: Rowdy went first, as his hunger to conquer this skill grew with every attempt. Moody and I waited patiently and confidently, manning the starting flag and stopwatch (actually an old Timex pocket watch). I'd drop the flag and the "Hare Pair" would explode off the line.

They covered ground at a remarkable rate as they drew nearer and nearer to the target post. This is precisely where their problem always arose. Ginger was always enthusiastic about running, but somewhat less so when it came to stopping. Normally Rowdy would wait too long to start his attempt at slowing her and would end up with a very tough shot at his target. It was made more difficult because instead of roping the post straight on, as was desired, he was forced to guess which way Ginger would turn when she realized she was going to run head long into the fence. This decision occurred at exactly the same time, as he gauged how tightly to grip the saddle horn with one hand while flinging his loop with the other during this high-speed turn.

Many were the times he misjudged his grip and went rolling like a barrel under the boards of the fence. This dismount style did have some merit, as it was very rapid, but I always believed it lacked a certain amount of finesse.

Rowdy and Ginger would make their way back to the starting line dejectedly to hear their final time, man the start flag, and watch for Moody and me. Our runs went somewhat differently. Rowdy would drop the flag, and the "Tortoise Twins" would leave the line. Our ground coverage was somewhat less rapid, but steadily we loped along. Our advantage became extremely apparent as we neared the post. Moody was the greatest stopper ever. There was nothing I can remember that he ever enjoyed more. He'd lock up the brakes and always allow me a perfect straight-on shot at the rope post, and I seldom missed.

I'd fly off his back and attack the fence with reckless abandon. Five quick steps and I was at the top, three quick wraps and a hooey. I'm not sure to this day just exactly what a hooey is, but that was what the rodeo announcers always said, so that's just what we did.

We would then wait the traditional five seconds to let the post try to free itself, and then we'd proudly return to the starting line. I think Moody and I were undefeated in that event.

Such was not the case with barrel doggin', as this was always the most hotly contested event of our rodeo. It was patterned after bull doggin'. Some less informed people refer to bull doggin' as "steer wrestling."

Barrel doggin' required speed, agility, and, most of all, guts. It ranks high as one of our most dangerous events. The object of the contest was to race by a prone steel fifty-gallon barrel, leap from your running horse onto it, and then roll it the entire length of your body. This roll signaled the end of time and, more than once, the end of the rodeo.

There were a few things about that particular event that could have brought about much pain. For instance, timing was very important. If you left your horse too early, you crashed to the ground; if you left late, you again crashed; but if you left at exactly the right moment, you landed on the steel barrel. Now that I think of it, everything about this event brought about a fair amount of pain. After landing "safely" on the barrel, one's focus was on the all-important roll over. This was an area where Rowdy and I had vastly different standards.

Rowdy's idea of a successful roll was rolling one end or the other up one leg, over his side, and off his shoulder, completely missing his head. He explained that as long as it rolled past his head, it was legal. I didn't argue, but knew my way was the much more professional approach. I was never satisfied with an attempt that didn't actually roll the entire length of my body.

I always believed that my style was the way the maneuver was meant to be. I'd stick the toes of my boots under the middle of the barrel and then grab both ends while falling backwards. As the barrel rolled up my legs and over my waist, I'd bridge quickly, sending the hapless creature over my chest and bouncing off my chin and forehead. I was always a believer in tucking one's chin during the bridge, as the barrel would sometimes become lodged on the jawbone, costing precious seconds.

Barrel doggin' was always the final event of our home rodeos, as it wore the horses pretty ragged in no time at all. Not to mention the contestants.

If anyone reads this story and has ideas of creating his or her own home rodeo, allow me to give some advice. Be creative, be careful, and above all, remember when barrel doggin', tuck that chin.

Chapter 6

TRICKS, HORSES, AND ROCK AND ROLL

In the days of my youth, Rowdy and I spent the majority of our time on horseback. Subsequently, we were both very accomplished riders by the tender ages of three years old. This gift enabled us to accomplish far greater things aboard a horse than the traditional sitting and staying on. We were constantly on the lookout for new tricks to perform atop our trusty steeds, and fortunately we were blessed with our wild Aunt Kelly, whom it seemed had a never-ending supply.

Our house at the time was less than a mile across a large hayfield away from our grandparents, and consequently from our crazy aunt Kelly's. Kelly was only three years older than Rowdy and had to be one of the youngest aunts of all times. Rowdy and I always thought of her more as a sister, but better, as we could send her home if she got too bossy or gross. Such as the time she drew big kissy lips on the croquet mallets and pretty much demanded that we marry them. We left.

Most of the time she was good company, and there were very few things she wasn't willing to try on a horse. Kelly rode bareback probably eighty percent of the time and, due to that, was an excellent rider. Even so, she did spend her fair share of the time face first in the dirt.

Kelly's horse, Stormy, was a Pony of America (P.O.A.) breed and was several hands taller than our Shetlands. She was a black and white paint, and Kelly thought she was the most beautiful and smartest horse in the world. She spent countless hours braiding her mane and tail or teaching her some fancy new trick to impress us with. She had many, many tricks. She had the standard Run Up From Behind and Vault Over Your Horse's Rear and Onto Its Back down to a science. That is, if Stormy was in the mood and didn't side step, leaving Kelly face first in the dirt. Either way, it was always fun to watch.

Kelly was also the first of our trio to try the very risky maneuver known as the Full Out Running Spin Around. This magnificent trick consisted of getting one's horse up to speed, dropping the reins, and then spinning around backwards. Kelly was without a doubt the master of that trick, and Rowdy and I held her in high regard for it.

One other trick that I should mention, as it, too, was very dangerous and exciting, was her patented Indian Style Fighting Trick. This trick was almost impossible for us to duplicate, as it required longer legs than we were blessed with at the time. Seems she'd seen a picture in a book that illustrated an Indian warrior hanging precariously off the side of his mount, using it as a shield while firing his weapon under the racing horse's neck.

To pull this off you had to have long enough legs to hold around your horse's back and belly while you squeezed its neck with your top arm and fired your weapon with the other. Thankfully, Rowdy and I were secure in the knowledge that we were cowboys and would never have use for this cowardly maneuver if war ever broke out.

Above all the tricks, however, there was one thing for which Kelly always had a passion. That one thing was racing. She wanted to race constantly. It was a nightly ritual to race across the big hayfield to the county road. It was on one of those nights that Kelly introduced us to The Beatles.

It was getting late one evening as we made our way out of the woods and down the lane toward the edge of the field. Kelly had been telling us about her research in the field of rock and roll and horse behavior. We, being country western buffs, were very skeptical. She was very insistent, so we agreed to hear her out.

It seemed that a group called The Beatles had recently come out with a song that contained a verse that went, "She loves you, ya—ya—ya." Kelly was convinced that this verse, if sung in the proper key, could actually increase a horse's speed tenfold. Rowdy and I agreed that it was a far-fetched idea, but decided that it was worthy of a try.

When we reached the field's edge, we pulled up into a line and prepared for the big race. Preparing for the race consisted of looking for signs of movement around our parents' barns to make sure no one was watching, as this nightly race was strictly forbidden. Everyone knows letting horses run home ruins them for life, after all.

Seeing no one looking, we turned our eyes to Kelly, as she was the official starter. A wild look came into her eyes, and her face contorted hideously as she screeched out the word "Yeaaa!" And we were off.

"She loves you, ya—ya—ya!" We screamed louder and louder across the field. It must have been quite a sight. Stormy and Ginger bolted like shots from a gun, manes and tails whipping like shreds of a flag in a hurricane. Moody was somewhat less inspired by this Beatle mania and set off more like a large stone from a small sling shot, his mane and tail more resembling laundry in a spring breeze. It was on these nightly races that my dear horse's handicap of being "velocity challenged" really held us back.

I don't know who won the race, and I really can't say I remember anyone ever winning. I attribute this to the fact that my vantage point was never a favorable one for judging a photo finish. The only photo available was that of a couple of horses' rears disappearing into the distance . . . on their ponies.

I often wondered why Moody wasn't affected by that verse like the other two horses. I would later come to realize that females always did go a little psycho wherever the "Fab Four" were concerned.

Chapter 7

TO DINE OR KNOTS

It is said that a child's personality is almost completely developed by the time he or she is five years old. If this statement is indeed true, and I tend to believe it may be, it certainly could account for that nervous, wild-eyed look in my mother's eyes. It might also account for that strange nervous tick of my father's that compels him to grip any available eating utensil and wield it over his head like a club whenever I come to dinner.

Dinnertime, I am told, is a time for families to come together and share stories of the day's events, enjoy the cuisine de jour, and generally bond. Dinnertime at our house, as I recall, was somewhat different. I should point out that my memory of this subject may be somewhat sketchy, as usually about ten or fifteen minutes into this bonding period I would experience a temporary blackout—this a result of a knife handle coming into contact with my neatly-shaved noggin.

You see, I was born with a gift (some say a curse) that compelled me to say the exact wrong thing at the worst possible moment. I say I was born with this gift/curse because, hard as I try, I can't remember ever doing it deliberately or even trying to cultivate this skill; it was just there. I say *was* because I believe that as I've grown older and wiser I've learned control it. My wife says not, but she's just stupid. Oops.

The dinner table, it seemed, was the place that my gift/curse most often surfaced, and this was unfortunate, considering the proximity of available bludgeons at my father's disposal. These factors, combined with Dad's stringent guidelines for appropriate table behavior, made dinner one of my least favorite times of the day. Dad was a strong believer in good table manners, and to his credit, I believe that by the time I moved out of the house I would have felt comfortable dining with the Queen of England, herself. Some of the rules of the table were as follows: no singing, no whistling, humming, horsing around, loud or abrasive talk, laugh attacks, and most certainly, NO GAGGING WHILE LOOKING AT THE NIGHT'S MAIN COURSE.

My gift/curse never seemed to bother Rowdy and, in fact, on many occasions he was actually able to use it to his advantage.

Dinner at our house usually went something like this: The family sat down to dinner promptly at six p.m. Dad, who had worked his tail off all day loading boxcars with lumber, would take his place at the head of the table. I would sit directly to his right, Rowdy at the other end, and my mother on his left. Many were the times I lobbied to change the seating arrangement, but sadly to no avail. The moment of sit down was always a critical point, as this was the time we surveyed what was set before us to eat.

Dad would usually smile at Mom and say something nice like, "Looks good, hon," or something equally sappy.

I, on the other hand, might be overcome with the gift/

curse and say something like, "Yuck, that gravy looks like dog barf!" A distinct ringing in my ears nearly always followed a comment like that—and the uncontrollable urge to scratch the growing knot on my head. When my eyes uncrossed, I could always count on them focusing on my father, knife in hand, asking why I would say such a foolish thing.

"Someone had to say it," I'd blubber, and dinner was officially under way.

Someone had to say it was, and still is to this day, the only rationale I am able to offer for any wacky, tasteless, or uncalled for comment that may slip from my mouth. It always seemed reasonable enough to me, but unfortunately not everyone buys into that line of thinking.

Rowdy did buy into it, however, and, in fact, it seemed to me that he was always a little in awe over some of the gems I would blurt out. This was great for me, as there was very, very little that I ever did that Rowdy felt even the slightest bit awed by. Normally it was the other way around.

"How do you do that?" he'd ask after dinner while inspecting my latest knot.

"What?" I'd ask, thinking he was referring to my ability to cross my eyes so far that they would actually change sockets or my ability to grow knots the size of Mount Vesuvius.

"Just blab anything that pops into your thick little head," he'd say while measuring and charting the size, type, and location of my knot in his knot log.

"Just a gift, I guess," I'd say, my chest puffing out with pride.

As I made mention before of my brother being able to use my gift/curse to his advantage, allow me to share with you an example. Let's say, just for argument sake, that we were able to get through the sit down phase of dinner without my being compelled to comment on the origin, coloration, or texture of the food set down before us, and the next phase of dinner would begin. Plate filling.

My parents come from a time when if it was on the table, presented as food, it was edible. As such, it was required that everyone had *some* of everything available. The amount was negotiable, and you were given two options: that of taking a reasonable amount yourself or letting Dad determine a reasonable amount for you. Since Dad's idea of reasonable was anything but that, option number one was always the only true choice.

Bear in mind one very important detail. Once something resembling food was on one's plate, it was expected that it would then be eaten, completely. That is why proper apportionment was so important, and also one's ability to guess whether what *looked* good actually *tasted* good. Gravy was always tough. Sometimes it looked good, but tasted gross, and sometimes it looked like dog barf, but was actually quite tasty. Gravy was where Rowdy always chose to play the gift/curse card.

"Try the gravy," he would whisper, nudging me under the table with his foot.

"I don't think so," I'd say, shooting a quick glance in Dad's direction.

"Looks good," he'd say. "Probably burger in those lumps."

"Burger? Mmmm," I'd say, "maybe I *will* try it."

My ability to apportion gravy was poor, and it seemed I always ended up with a plate full. Rowdy would sit and watch quietly as I'd dip my fork into the concoction. His eyes would grow large as my mouth closed slowly around my fork, knowing that soon there would be no doubt as to the edibility of the gravy du jour. If the lumps were indeed burger, as advertised, the reaction was minimal; a simple full-mouth smile and head nod told all that was needed, and Rowdy safely spooned gravy on his potatoes.

On the other hand, if the lumps turned out to be anything else, the reaction was dramatically different. I'd shut my eyes tightly and tears would stream down my cheeks as I squirmed wildly in my chair, trying to will the horrid mixture down my now constricted throat. If I did—you guessed it—someone had to say something, if for no other reason than to save the rest of humanity from the fate that I now faced: an entire plate of dog barf staring up at me waiting to be eaten completely.

"So, Mom," I'd choke, "exactly when did you decide that chopping up slugs and putting them into gravy was a good idea?"

CRACK. RINGGGGG.

"Rowdy, would you like some gravy for your potatoes?" Mom would ask.

"No thanks, Mom. Butter's just fine."

Chapter 8

TALKIN' COWBOY

Growing up as cowboy kids affected nearly every aspect of our young lives. We dressed like cowboys, we rode like cowboys, and finally, we talked like cowboys. How, you may wonder, do cowboys talk? It's not easy to explain.

Be warned, talkin' cowboy is something that cannot be learned from a textbook or self-help class at the local college. It is similar to the way a person takes a French class in school, then goes to France and makes an utter fool of himself. It is more something you develop from your first utterances and grows your whole life. I was fortunate enough to be born into a cowboy-speaking family. I've always felt very lucky for this and have spent a good portion of my life trying to help the less fortunate avoid blatant acts of gunselry.

Gunsel has always been a staple of a cowboy language. Gunsels, by definition, encompass a vast array of the population. They are the guys who see a cowboy on TV or in movies and decide they want to be one. This is a grave offense, as one can't just buy boots and a hat and suddenly become a cowboy. This same poor misguided soul runs out and buys a genuine Stetson and the highest, brightest, pointiest Acme boots at Joe Blow's Western World. He pops the Stetson high on his head and pulls the pointy boots onto his feet, tucking his pant legs neatly inside the tops. This pitiful man is at that moment a bona fide gunsel, and as such he has willingly sacrificed himself as the butt of all cowboy jokes and overall scorn among true cowboys.

A gunsel, in his quest to portray a cowboy, will even sometimes go so far as to try to talk like one. He goes to the library and gets a book on cowboys and sets about boning up on catch words like rodeo, lariat, chaps, and Brahma. These words are some of the most misused, mispronounced terms in the cowboy language. What a real cowboy calls a [ro-de-o] is pronounced [ro-day-o] by a gunsel. A lariat is a rope pronounced [rope], but a gunsel calls it a [lar-e-et]. Chaps are properly pronounced [shaps]. The gunsel's version of chaps is what true cowboys acquire after a long, hot day of riding a hard saddle. Lastly, this brings us to Brahma. This simple word, properly pronounced [bray-ma] caused me more cold shivers as a child than any other in the English language. Seems all gunsels, who included many of my schoolteachers, insisted on mispronouncing this word. They all felt, and maybe still do, that the word was pronounced [bra-ma]. Try as I might, it seems I could never get through to many of them. Sadly, gunsels inevitably spawn more gunsels, and now they are rampant in our society.

Fortunately, over the course of the past few years, helped by the advent of televised rodeos, the new generation of gunsels has become a little less conspicuous. You don't often have to deal with a pants tucker anymore, but there are still many store shelf Stetson wearers running around. I should point out that there is nothing actually wrong with a Stetson hat. The hat, itself, is of pretty good quality, but the problem comes in shape.

Most hats, especially those of the felt variety, are designed to be steamed and shaped to fit the wearer's personality or style. Gunsels never do this and so go through life with a stiff, shapeless blob of felt perched on their pointy heads. I pity these poor wretches more than anything else and will go on trying to save these folks from themselves till I die.

Sadly, my children weren't able, at first, to distinguish a cowboy from a gunsel, as I had hung up my boots and hat long before their births. (I was always a believer that if one did not have a horse, and did not ride, then one had no business wearing boots or hats. So when I sold my last horse and became citified, they went into the closet and have not been seen again.) I remedied this situation after I had a nightmare that still makes me break out in a cold sweat.

In this horrible dream, my kids walked into the house sporting shapeless Stetsons and pointy, shiny Acme boots with pants tucked in. They went on to tell me they were now cowboys/cowgirls just like when I was a kid. They said they were going to the ro-day-o to watch bucking broncos and Brama bulls. At this point I woke up screaming in the night and vowed to teach my kids the real way to talk cowboy.

Chapter 9

BAZOOKA MADNESS

It was the sixties. Late sixties, probably '68. I'd have to ask my father to be sure, for he is always sure about these things, but it may be of no consequence to the story except to try to rationalize my own struggle with addiction. It was, after all, the *sixties*.

Hippies and lawlessness were the rule of the land in those days, but substance abuse was not limited in its grasp to purely hippies, as this shocking tale shall reveal. This is the story of my personal walk on the dark side of madness: Bazooka Madness.

I had just turned seven years old that May and seemed on my way to becoming a fine young cowboy. I had the clothes: boots by Justin, jeans by Wrangler, and a snazzy button-up stiff collar shirt, probably from Anthony's. (Hey, we weren't rich.) I had the swagger, crew cut hair à la Mom, and most importantly, a custom fit and tailored Resistol straw hat, just like Dad's.

My life was full. I had my horse, and I had my older

brother, Rowdy, whom had convinced me by this stage in my life that he was indeed the all-knowing, all-seeing mighty one. And I had my infant brother who served as a good diversion for my mother.

The family was at a rodeo in Cranbrook, British Columbia, one fateful weekend that shaped up to be the same as any other such excursion. Saturday afternoon found Rowdy and me bored. We had already checked out the grounds, the condition of the stock, and, of course, whether Debbie McGhee had made the trip. Rowdy said it was important that we know that, and since he was all-knowing . . .

As we sat in the shade of a huge Ponderosa Pine, chewing on weeds and watching people buy snacks at the concession stands; we were witness to a most remarkable event. We both keyed in on a pudgy gunsel boy waddling toward the stand. In his hand was an empty Pepsi bottle. There was nothing remarkable about that, as this lad looked as if he liked his Pepsi. However, when he handed the empty bottle to the lady at the counter, she promptly deposited five pieces of Bazooka Bubble Gum in his waiting paw. Rowdy and I looked on with amazement.

"Bazooka for bottles? What a racket!" Rowdy piped up.

"I want some of that," I replied—and we were on our way toward madness.

In the beginning the bottles and, of course, the Bazooka came easily. It wasn't long before we each had stocked twenty or thirty pieces of gum. But sadly, with abundance comes waste and overindulgence.

I shudder to think how I must have looked then. Eight pieces of Bazooka stuffed into my swollen cheek, slobbering like a rabid dog, my shirtfront stained of drool. From my hat brim hung dried pieces of gum, remnants of gigantic bubbles. It must have been pathetic.

Chewing as we were, at the rate of ten pieces per hour, it wasn't long before our stashes of Bazooka were running dangerously low. Our nerves were becoming nearly as frayed as the roofs of our mouths as we each stared dejectedly at our nearly empty bags. The feeling of desperation enveloped me as I searched in vain for more pop bottles. There just were no more, it seemed, and no more bottles meant no more Bazooka. No more Bazooka Joe comics, no more reason to live. Bazooka Madness, you see, had me securely in its clutches. And so we searched and searched and searched, but found no bottles.

"Have people just stopped drinking pop?" I snapped at Rowdy as we both flopped down at the base of a tree. "Maybe that pudgy gunsel boy is hiding all the empties so only he can get the Bazooka! I say we hunt him down like the dog that he is and make him tell us where he has put the bottles!"

As my madness grew with every passing moment, I had to have it. I needed the smell of the sugar when you first peel the wrapper from the piece of gum. I needed the taste when you first pop it into your mouth with a flood of saliva and sweetness. And maybe, most importantly, how could I get through life without the wisdom gained by reading the Bazooka Joe comic that accompanied each delicious piece?

I believe it was somewhere around this point that Rowdy realized that something was terribly wrong with this picture. Perhaps he got a good look at me sitting there, mouth slightly agape, a look of horror, rage, and desperation on my gum-riddled face as I contemplated where my next piece of gum might come from.

"Robb, you want this way too much," Rowdy said seriously as he reached over and picked a piece of dried gum off the brim of my hat. "We should get going. The rodeo's going to start pretty soon, and Mom's going to wonder where we are if we don't check in," Rowdy continued as he rose to leave.

"Go?!" I shouted. "Just like that?! We can't just *go*, or maybe you don't remember—I HAVE NO BAZOOKA!"

Rowdy glared at me with disapproving eyes and simply stated, "I'm going with or without you," and then he turned and walked away.

"Just one more piece! Wait, just one more, just one!" I cried out after him, but he just turned and gave me a scornful look. He slowly shook his head and walked on.

So I was alone or, as alone as one can be at a public spectacle.

People scurried about, most in a hurry to get to events or to the grandstands, but I cared nothing of them. I wandered about the grounds, searching for the increasingly scarce pop bottle, which was the key to my next Bazooka fix.

My mouth had become incredibly dry as a result of all the previous drooling and I headed for a water fountain. I had just taken a drink and was standing upright, my cheeks still puffed with water, when my wide eyes beheld a magnificent sight. There, not twenty feet away, sat no less than twelve empty Pepsi bottles, neatly stacked in their original cartons. My mind raced. It was the classic battle of self, choosing between right and wrong. What I needed came to me: *justification.* That being, I quickly calculated. Number one, I needed Bazooka. Number two, I needed bottles. Number three; there were bottles twenty feet away. Number four, the bottles were stacked neatly so someone, perhaps the owner of the camper they're stacked beside, *wants* the bottles returned anyway, and I would actually be doing them a favor. Surely that was the case, I rightly decided, and the thought did cross my mind to walk right up to the camper and ask. I say, the thought did *cross* my mind, it just didn't stop. It just kept right on crossing as I inched my way closer and closer to the bottles. I could hear people talking on the other side of the camper as I came into grabbing distance of my intended quarry. Slowly and carefully I latched onto the handles and was turning to make my getaway when the pudgy gunsel boy sounded the alarm. There was the clatter of glass, a tiny dust trail, and the echo of distant Justin boots as I did my best Road Runner imitation, six packs flapping in the wind at my sides. I didn't stop till I was far away and well hidden.

The emotions I was experiencing were many, ranging from guilt to joy. I didn't know what to do next, but what I did know was that I'd been seen, and now there I was with twelve hot pop bottles in my possession worth about a billion Bazookas. It was clear to me that I had to get rid of those bottles, and the way I saw it I had two options. One was to return the bottles to their rightful owner, explain the circumstances, and beg for mercy. The other was to take the bottles to the concession stand and trade them for enough Bazooka to last a month.

As I approached the counter, my heart nearly beat out of my chest. The lady standing behind the counter looked at me somewhat suspiciously, I thought, as I presented her the bottles and reached out my trembling hands.

"Let me get you a bag for that, young man," she said accusingly, I thought. I snatched the bag from her, held it low and close to my body so as not to draw attention to myself, and set off to get away from the probing eyes of all those people around the concession stand. As I made my way toward the arena, I stayed low and out of the open as much as possible, always scanning the crowd in search of the pudgy gunsel boy and the Pop Bottle Posse that I was sure had been formed by this time.

I had just popped around the corner of a horse barn when I felt someone grab my collar. Instantly my tear ducts went into overdrive as the realization came to me that crime doesn't pay, and all the Bazooka in the world wasn't worth the torture I'd been going through these past couple hours. I was babbling something to that effect when my eyes cleared long enough to make out the form of Rowdy standing beside me with his hand on my collar.

"Where have you been?" he demanded. "I've been looking all over for you!"

Again I broke down as I told him the whole sordid story and how I was now a fugitive, and he, by association, was now harboring a fugitive. Rowdy furrowed his brow and pondered the problem we now faced. Fortunately, he was all-knowing, and it didn't take him long to come up with a plan. His plan, I would find out, would only cost me slightly more than half of my precious Bazooka, but I was glad to pay it. Rowdy assumed his patented "Very Wise" stance, with his right elbow tucked neatly in his left palm, and his chin resting in his right palm.

"As I see it, the only thing still linking you to the crime is the bag and the Bazooka. Now, while the gum is in the bag, it is what is called public domain," he went on, doing his best imitation of Perry Mason. "But by removing the gum from the bag and stuffing it in our pockets, it becomes private domain and can't be touched.

"Then," Rowdy went on to explain, "we just ditch the bag and walk away." He smiled, pleased with his reasoning, and set about dividing the contents of the bag into our pockets. Naturally, he, being older and larger, was able to carry the most pieces of gum in his pockets. To me it was a small price to pay to be out of the hangman's noose, and I gladly accepted the split, stuffing nearly a half billion pieces of Bazooka into my bulging pockets.

My addiction to Bazooka thankfully was short lived. It seems after a few days I came down with a rare form of lock jaw, which would not allow me to put a piece of gum remotely near my lips. Such an act would cause such cramping in my jaw muscles that I was not able to fit a single piece between my teeth.

 As I become older, of course, I realize that my brother's legal advice was only slightly twisted, but as I've said, it was the sixties.

Chapter 10

TAKING FLIGHT

Just because Rowdy and I were natural-born cowboys doesn't mean we lacked refinement in equestrian events. Show jumping (hay bales) aboard Moody and Ginger was always a terrific summer pastime. The trick here was not necessarily getting over the bale, but staying mounted at the same time. This proved to be a very worthy challenge much of the time. Since this sport required that the participants have no saddle, shirt, shoes, nor jeans—only cutoffs—the stakes were high. We first encountered this sport at a rodeo in Grangeville, Idaho. A group of Indian kids (This was long before the days of "political correctness.") gave a horse jumping show before the rodeo, and we knew then that we had to try it. We watched as they flew gracefully over barrier after barrier. No saddles, no shoes, and often times no hands! Needless to say, we were very impressed.

As soon as we got home, we began trying to figure out how to build barriers for our horses to jump. We realized our ponies were not going to make it over six-foot fence rails, so we looked for options available to us. Much to our delight, Grandpa had just bailed hay in the field next to our house. What more could we have hoped for: twenty-four-inch barriers as far as the eye could see. Some were even turned up on their sides for extra high jumps.

We hurried into the house to change into our flying Indian costumes. Cut-offs on and shoes off, we were dressed for the airways. We shouted to Mom that we were going riding. She replied with the traditional, "Okay, don't be long; be careful; look both ways," or something equally meaningless to us, and we headed for the barn.

Quickly we gathered the ponies and headed for the world hay bale jumping championships. I admit our first attempts at show jumping were less than awe-inspiring. At first we thought that by simply pointing the ponies at the barrier, their jumping genes would take over and compel them to gracefully take flight. Such was not the case. It seemed that my Moody's eating gene far overpowered his jumping one, and Ginger's dodge or stop gene took precedence.

After several failures (and hours probably), we had about decided that only true Indian ponies and true Indian kids were capable of the aerial acrobatics that we longed for. Rowdy and I found a shady spot under a large Ponderosa Pine and assumed our customary resting positions. The customary resting position was that of lying flat on our backs atop our horses, using their ample behinds as pillows while our ponies munched on loose hay left behind by the baler. On this particular day, we hadn't been there long when Rowdy was struck with inspiration.

"Those Indian ponies ran *all* the time!" Rowdy blurted as he came upright from his prone position on his horse. I was not immediately aware of the significance of what he was telling me and remained lying on my back with my head resting on Moody's soft rear end. It seems Rowdy had no time for explanation and headed off at a gallop.

Ginger galloped along gracefully and happily, glad to be getting to stretch out a little. They made a wide half-circle and galloped back toward my horse and me. I could see Rowdy was lining up a turned-up bale and gaining speed. As the duo moved closer and closer to the formidable barrier, I prepared myself for the landmark exhibition. And that it was. As Rowdy and Ginger reached the moment of truth, I was sure they could never overcome the horrible dodge gene that was so deeply in control of Rowdy's mount. Rowdy, to his credit, had factored in that variable also, because just as she started to balk, he let out the most blood curdling war whoop I had ever heard and firmly planted his bony bare heels into the stodgy horse's rib cage. Up and over the bale they went, soaring like eagles in the summer sky. Success at last.

Inspired by Rowdy's maiden flight, and the fact that once that first one was behind you it was smooth sailing, I set off for my own moment in the sun. I took the same route, a wide half-circle at an easy gallop. As we finished the turn, I let loose my grip on the reins and gave my steed his head, this was his signal to pick up speed, but it seemed he missed the signal, so I had to remind him by screaming like a banshee and pounding his sides with my bare heels. After a moment, he caught the drift and picked up momentum. I leaned forward over his withers to cut down on wind resistance and grabbed both handfuls of his long white mane. I could feel the steady pounding of his hooves and the rhythm of his breathing as we crossed the point of no return. Finally we would fly—and we did.

Inexplicably, Moody locked up the brakes at the last moment. Since I was doing my part to cut down wind resistance by leaning forward, this sudden change in momentum put me in somewhat of an awkward position. That being approximately half way up his neck, standing on my head. Just as I was resigning myself to flying over my horse's head and landing face first in stubble, Moody did a strange and marvelous thing. He jumped. Up came his head, and me, and away into the great blue yonder we flew. I can only imagine how majestic we must have looked. He flying over the enormous obstacle and me hanging from his sturdy neck, bare feet flailing in the air. The landing proved to be a little rough, as the jolt of the ground sent me rolling across the stubble field, but the flight was a success. We had gone over the bale together, and that was all that mattered. Later I came to learn that the element of surprise was by far the most reliable component in horse jumping. I found that if Moody didn't have a chance to think about what he was doing, he would just react and do what he had to do to survive and keep me alive.

As long as I live, I will never forget that little pony, or the many wonderful times we shared. His love for me was as simple and unconditional as mine was for him. I think about him often, and often it is at a time when I feel unsure or scared about some obstacle I have to face. And then I remember that day in the hayfield and realize that whatever the obstacle, there is only one way to face it. Head on. Thanks, Moody.

Chapter 11

CALF RIDIN'

As I sat down on the fiery beast, I could feel his muscles flex and ripple. As I felt the rope being pulled tight across my palms, I could feel the heat radiating from his wide back like a furnace. My heart beat at a torrential pace, and every ounce of my body was electric with anticipation. As I pulled down my old straw cowboy hat, I took a deep breath and said a silent prayer. I had waited my whole life for this moment and I knew I was ready. My dad, who served as my coach and mentor, rattled off last minute instructions. Lean back, stick your chest out, turn your toes out, lift on your rope . . .

I was five years old and riding my first calf at the Boundary County Fair. As a child, being a cowboy and going to rodeos all over the country, it only seemed natural that I would one day compete in the "Big Shows" just like Dad. Unfortunately, the only opportunity we got to hone our skills was at the fair. It was an event we, my big brother and I, looked forward to like Christmas. While we were able to get on the odd calf at my grandpa's or my Uncle Hap's place during branding, the fair was a whole different ball game. There were chutes involved, as well as fans. People would pack the stands to watch all manner of kids try their hands at calf riding. City kids, farm kids—heck, if we'd have had suburbs back then, we'd have had suburban kids lined up to give it a go.

Some, like Rowdy and me, did it for the passion; some did it on a dare; but, when it came right down to it, most did it for the shiny silver dollar that awaited each contestant as they picked themselves, or were picked, out of the arena's dirt. That's right, a shiny silver dollar to risk life and limb for our parents' entertainment. Not a bad deal, if you ask me. Most kids were much older than me that first year, and truthfully, most didn't believe me when they asked if I was going to ride. "Of course I'm going to ride," I'd say, squinting out from under the large brim of my well-worn hat. Dad was kind of in charge, or so it seemed to me. Of course, looking back, Dad was always in charge. He told me before we got there that he wanted me to wait till the second go-round to let some of the older kids go first. I remember being disappointed, but figured that would give me a chance to see the competition as well as the stock. Rowdy, as he always did, made an excellent ride, as I recall, garnering his first of many wins in his age group. He was undefeated in his career at the fair, which stretched over seven years. He was without a doubt the most naturally talented rider I ever saw.

Finally, after what seemed like an eternity, my calf sidled into the chute in front of me. He seemed huge, and he even had little horns sprouting out of the top of his white head. Dad slipped the rope into place, and I crawled down the old wooden chute side. Rowdy stood beside the chute, happily telling any onlooker who happened to ask, "Who is that little kid?" that I was indeed his brother. That made me feel good. I will say that there was a time when I wondered about the sanity of that endeavor, but I knew there was no turning back.

I'll take a brief moment to explain that "no turning back" reference. You see, growing up with my dad there were two things that a man, regardless of age or stature, never did. One was lie, and the other was quit. Rest assured there were plenty of kids that when the time came to actually get on their calf and nod for the gate to open fell apart and started crying like babies and bolted from the arena. This action constituted a lie, in that they said they were going to do something, and quitting, in that they quit before they ever started. Since the notion of facing my father after behaving in such a manner was far scarier than the prospect of being trampled into the dirt by a calf, I reasoned that there was indeed no turning back.

As I leaned back looking at the sky, sticking my chest out like a new marine recruit, I slowly turned the toes of my boots out, hooking into the loose skin of the calf below me with my spurs. I could feel his rib cage moving in and out with every quick breath he took. Dad's voice was drowned out as the blood rushed to my head, and I gave the well practiced sign that I was ready. I nodded my head. I didn't actually see the chute open, but I felt the calf pivot beneath me. This was it. The calf made two small hops as he left the chute, which I handled without incident. His next jump, however, caught me off guard, throwing me back off my rope, and then forward, smashing my nose into the top of his head as he kicked up his back legs. My nose hurt, and I was way out of shape, but I wasn't letting go. The rest of the ride was somewhat of a blur, but I finished that ride lying on my belly on the calf's back, hanging on for dear life. I remember hearing the whistle and being afraid to let go of the rope. Then I did let go, and I can vividly remember hitting the ground and watching the calf's hind feet fly by me. The next thing I remember is looking up through blurry eyes and seeing my grandpa standing there with a shiny silver dollar. I felt an almost overwhelming sense of pride as I beat the dust off my Wranglers with my old hat. I could see my big brother smiling from ear to ear, clapping his hands and bragging to his buddies behind the chutes. I took my dollar from my smiling grandpa and placed it ceremoniously in my dirt-filled pocket. It was a very, very good day.

Was it worth it, you might wonder? Who knows? About all I can say is that the memory of that day in 1967 is one of the most vivid memories that I have. It is one of those defining moments that people talk about, I guess, that determines who you are and who you're going to be in the future. Did I become a professional rodeo cowboy? No. Did I ever again win the calf ridin' at the fair? No. Did I find a new closeness with my brother? Nah. Did I discover the ability to persevere even through pain and adversity? Nope. Rather, what I think I found was resolve.

Resolve to do my best, to make my family proud, and, of course, the resolve that still sees me through every working day. The fact is that on that day I resolved that I was willing to do almost anything for a buck.

Chapter 12

PRINTHETH AND FRECKLES

It is widely believed that pets, even horses, tend to take on their owner's personality after a time. In the case of Freckles Fullbottom and his horse, Princess, nothing could have been further from the truth. Freckles was about as close to a neighbor as Rowdy and I had while growing up, and as such he was one of the best friends we had at that point of our lives. He lived about a mile away from us across Nowland's field. Freckles had a dad who was a part-time calf roper. He went to one or two rodeos a year and spent the rest of the year endlessly recounting his fleeting brushes with glory. Freckles, being constantly exposed to this, had the warped image that his dad was the greatest cowboy on the face of the earth. We knew that this could not possibly be the case, since the greatest cowboy in the world just happened to live in our house. This cowboy was, in fact, my father, who rode bucking horses and bulls every weekend of every summer for some fourteen years.

Many times we tried to explain just how low on the

rodeo food chain calf ropers were positioned. All of our attempts seemed to fall on deaf ears, which was probably because Freckles talked constantly—and with a bit of a lisp to boot. Obviously, being good friends, Rowdy and I never let this unfortunate speech impediment hinder our enjoyment of his company. We simply never stood directly in front of him when he was speaking, so as to avoid the inevitable spit shower that accompanied many common words in our vocabulary, like "horses and sticks." He called his horse "Printheth." Try to say that without spitting. You get my point.

Like his dad, Freckles was also a part-time cowboy, just the kid version. He dressed, walked, and talked the part, but had one fatal flaw: Freckles was terrified of horses, even his own. This fact was of great concern to his father, who rightly determined that he would grow out of it. However, there were two large obstacles to overcome; one sat on Freckles' shoulders, and the other was somewhat south of there. That problem being Freckles' very round behind. Much like a Weeble on a rounded chair arm, he'd wobble a little, then just fall off. This always created much anguish.

When he would come to ride with us, the scenario was this: He'd saddle Princess, and then he'd set off across the field. He'd ride till he fell off or Princess gave him the sign that it was time to dismount, usually at about fifty to a hundred yards away. Her signal was convincing, I'll admit, as it consisted of her either getting spooked of her shadow and bolting to one side or, more dramatically, throwing up her head and rearing as high as she could, sending poor Freckles off of her backside and onto his. This nearly always resulted in a broken back, which was always Freckles' favorite injury. (Now obviously, Freckles never suffered an actual "broken back." Freckles was, however, a bit of what would now be referred to as a "Drama Queen," and this was his self-diagnosis in regard to almost any ache or pain he might endure.)

At this point Freckles dusted off, picked up the reins, and set off leading Princess toward our house. Usually we would agree to play guns, rodeo on stick horses, or something other than actual riding. One day was different though, and I won't forget it.

Freckles came limping into the yard one summer afternoon, as was his custom, with Princess in tow. A surprised, even horrified, look came across his round, freckled face as he saw us mounted and ready for a day of trail blazin'.

"I—I thought we might play gunth," he stuttered hopefully.

"Nope, not today, Freckles," Rowdy said matter-of-factly.

"Well, how about thtick hortheth?" Freckles groveled.

"No!" I said in my most stern six-year-old voice. "Today we really go riding."

Freckles' face was white as a sheet, and his bottom lip started to quiver ever so slightly. The jig was up. We shouted to Mom that we were leaving and waited patiently for the ever-present warnings, "Don't go too far; be careful; et cetera, et cetera." And then we were off.

We hadn't gone far when we realized Freckles was still leading Princess, his head hung in shame. Realizing we'd never get anything done waiting on these two, we doubled back, sporting our most scornful and disgusted looks.

"Freckles, git on that horse!" Rowdy demanded.

"I can't!" Freckles whined. "Sheth tired from coming clear acroth the field."

"Baloney!" I blurted. "You're chicken."

"Am not, you little frog!" He was three years older than me and didn't like being called chicken one bit.

"Then get on and let's go," Rowdy intervened.

"Okay," he said, "but if my horth goeth lame, ith your

fault."

Rowdy and I rolled our eyes at each other as Freckles scrambled and clawed his way aboard. We set out once again toward the lane that led to the woods. We made it about two hundred yards before Princess spooked at a dangerous looking plastic flag along the lane. She shot sideways, leaving Freckles suspended in the area where she had just been. He bounced as he hit the ground and started to howl.

"I broke my back! I broke my back!" he wailed. "Printheth, thath a bad, bad horth!"

Princess stood eating clover, not six feet from the awful plastic flag that had supposedly caused this calamity. She thought she was very smart.

We did our best to comfort our broken comrade and were able to determine that his back was not broken, probably just cracked or sprained, and got him to his feet.

"I want to go home," he sniffed.

"Wait, Freckles," Rowdy said. "I have an idea."

"I'll ride Princess. Robb can ride Ginger. And you can ride Moody."

I was in support one hundred percent, as my chances to ride my brother's horse were few and far between. Freckles reasoned that since he had a broken back, it probably would be safest if he went along with the plan. We switched our saddles around and soon were all remounted and on our way.

We'd gone another hundred yards or so when Princess decided she was tired of carrying a rider and threw her head up and stood tall on her back legs. Much to her surprise, when she came back to all fours, she still had a rider on her back. Even worse was the fact that now her head was pinned to the rider's knee and she was being forced to spin in a tight circle. She was mad and confused all at the same time.

Freckles' mouth hung open as he looked on, and for a brief

moment he was speechless—a very brief moment. "Printheth, thtop that!" he grunted. She didn't even look at him; she just stood stomping and blowing and shaking her head.

Rowdy casually stepped off, walked to the edge of the lane, and grabbed a stick that lay in the weeds. "She'd best not try that again," he hissed.

"What are you doin' with that thtick?" Freckles questioned.

"Maybe nothin'," Rowdy answered shortly as he swung himself back aboard Princess.

If that horse had any horse sense, she would have accepted the fact that she was bound to carry a rider all day and live with it. She didn't, and up she came again. This time her front feet weren't off the ground when she was stunned by a big stick crashing down between her ears. She shook her head and started up again. The stick came crashing down once again. This time she got the clue and was a perfect lady the rest of the day. We went on to have a great time that day, blazing trails and dining on peanut butter and pickle sandwiches. When we got back to the house, Mom came out to tell us that Freckles was very late and would probably be in deep dutch if he didn't get his fanny right home. We quickly put his own saddle back on his horse and said our goodbyes. To our amazement, he crawled up onto his saddle and headed off toward home. I believe it was the only time I ever saw Freckles in our yard, coming or going, on top of his horse. I can only imagine how proud Freckles and his dad must have been when he came riding into his yard on a very tired, probably still somewhat confused, Princess.

Freckles and Printheth . . . the epilogue:

The real person whom the character Freckles Fullbottom is based upon was, and is, a very dear friend to my brother and me. In truth, he did outgrow his fear of horses and, in fact, became an accomplished rider and roper later in life. He also outgrew the speech impediment that he had at the time, and now one is able to stand face to face with him and have a conversation without dodging droplets. Love ya, "Freckles."

Chapter 13
RODEO SCOUTS

"Yep," I drawled without peering out from under the brim of my old straw cowboy hat. "Old Speck is a rank old bull. You sure have got yer work cut out today," I went on. As I finished drawing a circle in the dirt behind the bucking chutes with the toe of my boot, I allowed myself to look upon the now pale face of the young cowboy who stood before me. I could tell the news I had given him was probably not what he was hoping for, as a thin bead of sweat appeared on his thin, somewhat trembling upper lip.

"What do you think I should look for?" he whispered in a hoarse voice as he glanced around nervously. I was sure he felt more than just a little self conscious about asking a six-year-old boy for advice. He needn't have, as most of the cowboys who followed the circuit had done the same at one time or another.

Rowdy and I, you see, prided ourselves on knowing every tendency or quirk of every rough stock animal in the McGowan Rodeo string. Being exceptionally entrepreneurial for our ages, it didn't take us long to realize that this ability could be most useful, and often times even profitable. For instance, we were always allowed behind the chutes during the rodeos, we held a prominent spot in all the pre- and post-rodeo tailgate gatherings, and we were generally looked upon as "one of the guys." This was all well and good, but often times the rewards showed themselves in a more tangible form—that form being the always-attractive form of Bazooka Bubble Gum, a six-pack of empty pop bottles, or even the occasional quarter, which to us represented no less than twenty-five pieces of Bazooka.

Most of the kids our age paid very little attention to the goings on of the rodeos, which most of them attended only because their dads were entered. Meanwhile, we watched every event, every rider, and every horse and bull each and every weekend of the summer. We made mental notes, as writing of any kind was strictly forbidden as a summer activity. We knew, for instance, that a bareback horse named Quicksand was what we called a money horse; she was the perfect draw in that event. We also knew that a saddle bronc named School Marm invariably treated her would-be riders to a urine shower almost every time out and that a bronc named Duster suffered from some sort of odd gastrointestinal problem, but was money for the right contestant. Of course, there were many, many more "less desirable" draws. For instance, a bareback named Papoose was the dirtiest, most unpredictable ding-a-ling in the string. Sometimes he would turn inside out, turning back, jumping and kicking, and looking like some kind of equine devil, and other times he'd act like the old plow horse after a hard day in the fields. Also, I remember a saddle bronc named Dull Knife, who had a reputation for rearing over backwards in the chute any time his potential rider would put his spurs in the points of his shoulders and ask for the gate to be opened. The trick with Dull Knife, you see, was to keep your feet down at his sides, nod for the gate, then when he turned to go out, quickly jam your spurs up to the points. He could be pure money, but he could also land you in the ambulance just as easily.

The horses were always good for a little payola, but honestly, the area that the payoffs were in was always the bull riding. It seemed like the vast majority of cowboy wannabes that showed up entered in bull riding. They were the easy marks, for they had no clue what to expect from the critter they had drawn, and by the time the day of the rodeo rolled around, they were usually questioning their sanity and looking for any help they could get. This was perfect for us, as the regular cowboys on the circuit were never very helpful and usually referred the newbies to us.

There were probably twenty bulls, and of those twenty, no two bucked or acted the same. Each had a very distinct personality and style.

Snowman, for instance, was the star of the show. The announcer always gave him the biggest build up, and he was the one who had never been ridden. We knew that story was about as much bull as old Snowman, himself, as we had seen him ridden. We understood that it was all part of the show, however, and went along with that in our scouting reports on him. "Oh, Snowman you say you've got," I'd say, slowly shaking my head from side to side. "Never been ridden, ya know." This was always extremely disheartening to my would-be clients, but it did provide an excellent opportunity to cash in. Looking out from under my hat, I would always follow up with this hook, "But, you do know there is a first time for everything, and I just might have some information you can use. . . ." This always set the cowboy to digging in their pockets or running to the concession stand for a bag of Bazooka.

Of course, the information that I would usually share was the same stuff, "He's gonna come out two jumps, turn back to the left, then back to the right. He's got a lot of power, so you want to beat him to the spot. . . ."

Sadly, most of Snowman's would-be riders seldom got to the turning back phase, as he was so big and powerful that, more often than not, he'd shoot them up like a cork out of a champagne bottle by the second jump. The nice part about Snowman, however, was that he was a most amiable sort. He had some impressive horns on him, but I never saw him use them. Apparently he never felt the need to further punish his adversary any more than was absolutely necessary.

This was not the case with some, however. Mohamed, for instance, was not a nice bull. I never was sure where McGowan picked this ill-tempered Brahma cross up, but presumably it was about the farthest point south of heaven. Mohamed's M.O. was usually pretty simple. He'd take four or five jumps out and to the right, all the while throwing power and belly rolls, then turn back to the left. Riding him was not the biggest problem, however, as many cowboys got him ridden. Getting off was another matter all together. You see, in four or five jumps, a cowboy finds himself a fair piece from the fence, or any sort of viable escape route, once he parts company with the bull. Mohamed knew this all too well, and he had a knack for knowing just where and when his opponent was going to hit the ground. I'll never forget the time he spun around on Dad and pinned him to the ground in Smelterville, Idaho. It was so quick that Dad never even had a chance to get up and moving before the bull was on top of him. I remember watching from the fence as Dad lay pinned between his horns and watching him kick the bull's front foot back every time Mohamed would try to stomp him. Fortunately, the clowns and the other cowboys were able to distract Mohamed long enough for Dad to get to his feet and make tracks for the fence.

The bull that the young cowboy was asking about, Speck, was indeed as tough to ride as I had let on to my perspective client. He was a large gray bull with, as his name would imply, some dark colored spots or specks scattered about his ample body. I knew the bull well, as he had been part of McGowan's string for a long time, but this was not the kind of information that came cheap.

I pulled my small hand from the pocket of my Wrangler jeans and held it out in front of me in a manner that could not be mistaken for anything other than what it was, a sign to put up or shut up. The pale-faced mark gazed at my outstretched hand, and then back at my steely six-year-old eyes. He seemed hesitant to comply at first, but when I dropped my hand, shook my head, and started to walk away, I broke him.

"Hey," Pale Face said, once again making a quick look around, "how much are you askin'?"

"Well," I said smugly, "that just depends on how much you want to know." Needless to say, he went for the entire deluxe package, to the tune of fifty cents, double the normal going rate because of his hesitancy.

As I sat on the fence rail later that afternoon, resembling a chipmunk with five or six pieces of Bazooka stuffed in my mouth, I watched my young protégé straddle Speck's broad back.

"How do you think he'll do?" Rowdy asked between bubbles.

"Well, he knows what to expect," I drawled. "Funny thing though," I added, blowing a Bazooka bubble as big as my head, "he never did think to ask what to do about it."

"Guess we'll just have to save that for next time," Rowdy chuckled as we watched Pale Face do a double back flip with a half twist on the second jump out of the gate.

Robb and Rowdy, Moody and Ginger - Circa 1965

"Cowboys, hat to boot tip…"

TRICKS, HORSES, AND ROCK AND ROLL

Boundary County fair parade
All decked out circa 1968

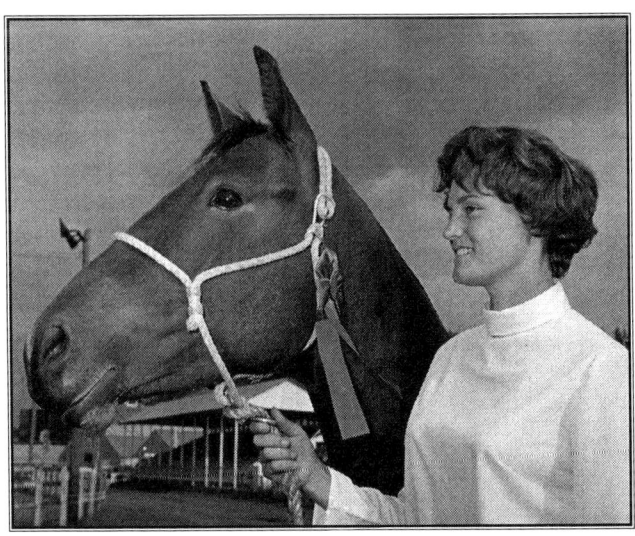

Mom and her horse Polly Ann Jordan
The fastest horse in north Idaho

Dad, around 1971, ready for the "show"

TRICKS, HORSES, AND ROCK AND ROLL

Rowdy and me hamming it up in the "big city"

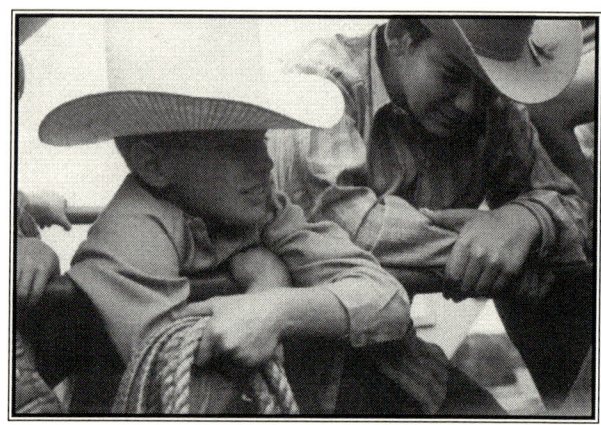

*Calf rope in hand waiting my turn to ride
Boundary County fair 1968*

Had him right where I wanted him! My first calf ride at the fair.

Had me right where he wanted me! Several years later.

Backpacking done right.

Me and Rowdy with dinner at Big Fisher Lake

My Grandpa and Grandma Wallace in the "good old days".

Chapter 14
NAME GAME

April 2, 1968, was a day in my life much like any other—except for one glaring difference. It seems sometime during the previous night, my mom had rendezvoused with a stork and picked up the newest member of the MacDonald family, my little brother.

This event didn't come as much of a surprise to Rowdy or me, as for months our parents had been preparing for the new addition. Mom and Dad were both sure that the stork would mercifully bring them a girl this time around, and they went so far as to pick out only girl names. Since the very idea of having a sister repulsed Rowdy and me, the responsibility of coming up with a suitable name for our new brother fell to us.

We, being up for most any challenge, set about weeding out viable options. Some of the front runners were:

Matt - as in Matt Dillon from our favorite TV show at the time (*Gunsmoke*)
Festus - as in Festus, also from *Gunsmoke*
Trampis - also from a popular TV show at the time

(*The Virginian*)

Charlie - as in Charlie Pride, the country western singer

We weighed the pros and cons of each prospect and tried to gauge each one's appropriateness. The process of testing each potential name involved repeating each name over and over to try to get a feel for how it might sound. It went something like this:

"Matt, Matt, Matt."

"Matt, Matt MacDonald."

"Matt Mac."

"Matt Donald."

"Matt, Matt Donald."

"Matt-Till-Da! Aaaargh! No good. Throw that one out. I'm not having any brother named Matt-Till-Da!"

"Festus, Festus, Festus."

"Festus MacDonald."

"Fester—oooh! Fester, pus—ick, no way!"

"Trampis, Trampis, Trampis."

"Tramp."

"Tramp piss . . . Mooom, Rowdy said piss!"

Slug. Ouch. And so on.

And so it was that we decided on Charlie and proudly revealed this selection to our parents. They seemed a little puzzled, and perhaps even a little amused by our choice, but nonetheless, they stood by their word that if the baby was indeed a boy, Charlie would be his name.

That night as Rowdy and I lay in our bunk beds going over the events of the day, and plotting out the next day, Rowdy became silent. I lay still in the darkness and awaited the words of wisdom that I was sure would follow his moment of silence. Sure enough, in about a minute—which was about the standard time it took for Rowdy to find wisdom—I saw his head pop over the edge of his top bunk.

"Robb," he whispered, "what do you really think of Charlie for a name?"

I gave my expected reply, saying, "I dunno. What do you think, oh wise one?"

"It might be kinda dumb," he said. "I think we better keep looking."

"Me too." I agreed. I always agreed.

As fate would have it, the next morning was Saturday, the only day of the week that we controlled our sixteen-inch black and white TV. It was Cartoon Day.

As we watched, we stayed alert for possible names for our new list, but since Daffy, Buggs, and Elmer were inappropriate for any cowboy, or most humans, we maintained our vigil. Just when we were beginning to believe that there were no suitable names, a commercial came on our small screen. The commercial featured a clown, complete with big red shoes, a huge painted smile, and burgers clutched in both gloved hands.

He skipped across a parking lot, and then stopped in front of some large arches, the biggest M we had ever seen. The announcer continued to babble about something as the clown proceeded to hop into a craft that was shaped like a giant hamburger and, much to our amazement, *flew* away. The announcer kept on talking as the burger flew into the distance, mostly gibberish to us, but his final sentence struck us like a lightning bolt. He ended the commercial by saying, "Come with Ronald McDonald and his flying hamburger to McDonalds."

We shot each other a quick glance, our eyes wide with excitement, and began to mumble.

"Ronald, Ronald, Ronald."

"Ronald MacDonald."

"Ron, not bad."

"Ronny—eegh—it'll do."

"That's it!" we shouted.

Ronald MacDonald and his flying hamburger! It was just too good to be true.

We ran and told Mom about the change in plans. She smiled and told us how creative we were, but cautioned us about getting too worked up because the new baby's name was going to be Kendra. Rowdy and I scrunched up our noses and made motions as if sticking our fingers down our throats.

I wondered what the matter with my mom was; she had always seemed pretty sensible up to this point. Personally, I attributed her clouded reasoning to the excess weight she had been packing on over the last six months in preparation for the visit from the stork. I must admit that I couldn't understand why the stork demanded that she be so fat and miserable just to get another baby. It seemed just plain cruel to me, but Mom never seemed to mind much.

As it turned out, we were right, and the stork dropped off a bouncy baby boy.

Mom and Dad were so stunned by the foresight we boys had shown in recognizing the gender of the baby that they did the only thing they could do.

On April 2, 1968, at Bonners Ferry Community Hospital, Ronald James MacDonald joined the family. We didn't get the flying hamburger, but, rest assured, we did get quite a clown.

Chapter 15
4-H CAMP

I pledge my Head to clearer thinking, my Heart to greater loyalty, my Hands to greater service, and my Health to better living, for my club, my community, and my country. So goes the 4-H pledge, and much like the Pledge of Allegiance, it has stuck in my mind for all of these years.

Four-H was a very big part of my early life, as aside from rodeos and saddle club meetings, it was a rare chance to get away from home. None of the other activities that our family took part in, however, offered my brother and me the opportunity to escape the surly bonds of parental intervention as did a glorious week during the summer known to us as 4-H camp. This much anticipated event took place in a location presumably inaccessible to parents and promised an entire week of hanging out with other kids, swimming, hiking, doing crafts of all sorts, and sleeping in genuine log cabins with rows of bunk beds from one end of their stout frames to the other. Believe you me, this all sounded like some kind of a kid paradise to a young man of nine years.

The year was 1971, and as the month of July rolled around, my anticipation of my first trip to 4-H camp grew to epic proportion. I had heard all the stories from the older kids I knew about the myriad of spectacular events available during this time. Carefully, I filled out my itinerary sheet, taking great care to sign up for all the activities that sounded like the most fun. Two choices in particular jumped out at me as being things that I would really enjoy and probably be good at. As I always considered myself to be particularly "artsy," I was extremely excited about the opportunity to do some "tie-dying" and "soap carving." Now I say that I considered myself to be "artsy," however, as I look back, I really should have taken into account the fact that I was never in any way shape or form "artistic."

Finally the day came that it was time to catch the bus to camp. Mom, I recall, was not nearly as sad to see my brother and me depart as I had pictured in my mind's eye. Rather, she seemed practically giddy as Rowdy and I grabbed our duffel bags and climbed aboard the big yellow bus. The bus ride was long and hot, as air conditioning consisted of rolling down thirty or forty windows on the bus and letting ninety plus degree wind blow through the confines of the rolling sardine can. I dreamed of the cool waters of Lake Whatchamacallit as sweat rolled over my forehead, knowing that soon I would be frolicking parentless in its crystal clear waters.

Upon arrival, we filed off the bus and were directed by the camp counselors to our assigned cabins. Rowdy and I were to stay in "Adams" cabin, which apparently was the most coveted lodging available. I dragged my duffel to the little log structure, taking in all the sights and sounds of my very first camp experience. After the long hot ride on the bus, I was eager to rid myself of my encumbrances (and clothes) and head for the cool clear waters of the lake. Unfortunately, I would suffer my first disappointment with 4-H camp in rapid fashion. It seems there were appointed times at which campers were allowed to frolic in the shimmering waters, and immediately upon first arrival was not one of them. Rowdy filled me in on the basics of camp behavior, which struck me as being perhaps a little too much like I had previously envisioned prison. He explained that we would be told when we could swim, when we could eat, when we had to go to bed and get up, and when we could explore the limitless abundance of our heretofore untapped artistic talents. Suddenly, I was finding 4-H camp to be a lot like home.

The first evening at camp was set aside for what was called "orientation." We met in front of the "mess hall" and were given the lowdown on everything from lights out to reveille and were apprised of the consequences for misbehavior. Around this time I began to wonder if coming on this trip was indeed such a good idea. The idea of appearing before a kangaroo court, and the punishment that such a tribunal could lay down, was daunting to say the least. I must have been visibly shaken, as Rowdy slapped my sweat covered back at the conclusion of the counselors' diatribe and assured me that it would be okay. "Just mind your manners," he said cheerfully as he exited to line up for "chow."

"Manners?" I thought to myself. "I thought this was supposed to be fun."

The mess hall did little to soothe my nerves, as half way through dinner some poor soul was forced to sing some sort of 4-H song in front of the entire group. The older kids laughed and made fun as this poor kid struggled to get through the mysterious melody. I was terrified that surely I would be the next target of this hazing and would no doubt have to appear before the kangaroo court for my failure to know any 4-H songs whatsoever. By some stroke of luck, I was spared, and when we were informed we could return to our cabin, I was but a streak across the yard. Safely inside the cabin, my stomach churned like a locomotive, and I wasn't really sure if it was nerves or the mystery stew I had just consumed. I knew one thing for certain, however: I wanted to go home.

That evening as darkness fell over the camp and the cabin began to fill up in preparation of "lights out," it dawned on me that I was residing in a cabin with a bunch of strangers, many of whom were much older, larger, and more seasoned campers than myself. I was not sure that I would ever be able to sleep in these conditions, nor before the night was over was I at all certain that I would even survive. When everyone was in the cabin and the door was closed (and presumably locked from the outside), one of the older kids whom had taken charge of our cabin did roll call. Names boomed from his overly developed maw, and he would lower his roll sheet to glare at each person answering with the customary "Here" to make sure that someone hadn't sneaked out and hired somebody to answer for them. I shuddered to think if some fool had ever done this, as kangaroo court would have been the least of his worries. After the roll was called and everyone was accounted for, our cabin leader explained his list of expectations of those of us lucky enough to share his dwelling. There would be no sneaking out, no talking after he'd made his final declaration of sleep, and no cabin raids without his express written consent and involvement. Finally, he said that if anyone snored and woke him up, he would hang them by their thumbnails from the rafters. I looked slowly at the rafters, then at my trembling thumbnails, and I can't remember ever feeling more ready to go home. You see, I snore. Not just a little, but I have been told throughout my entire life that I snore excessively. I looked frantically at Rowdy, who simply waved it off as nothing. "Just don't go to sleep until you know he's sleeping," he whispered. "He sleeps like a log, so he'll never know."

The lights went out, the declaration was made for everyone to go to sleep, and I lay in my little bunk listening to the even sounds of my co-tenants breathing as they drifted off to dream land. I, on the other hand, couldn't have slept with a handful of sedatives. I tossed and turned as images of things like cabin raids and swinging helplessly from the rafters by my thumbnails tumbled endlessly through my mind. Eventually I must have nodded off, succumbing to the stress of the day's events. I was awakened horrifically as there was a scream of terror from the bunk next to me. Seems our leader had pounced upon this poor hapless creature thinking his snoring had woke him up from his slumber. The poor guy was rousted around unmercifully and was given an atomic wedgie before he was told in no uncertain terms that he had better knock off the snoring or he'd be sleeping underneath the cabin with the packrats. I don't believe I slept for the rest of the week.

After the initial day and night, aside from not sleeping, I seemed to fall into the camp routine. I made a couple of new friends, and together we managed to get into just enough mischief to keep things fun, but to keep us out of kangaroo court. One night I was even involved in a "raid" of a neighboring cabin. Since I was largely nocturnal by this time, it was nice to have something to do with my spare time. Raiding, it turns out, was not nearly as dramatic as our leader had made it sound. After much planning and plotting, we simply burst into the cabin door at about one thirty in the morning, making all sorts of racket and pelting the still slumbering souls with pine cones. Then, in a moment of brilliance by our esteemed leader, he shouted "Adam's cabin rules!" leaving no doubt who the mysterious raiders had been. Needless to say, within a couple of nights we were the victims of a cabin raid. This turned out to be one time it was fortunate that I had forsaken sleeping because I heard the perpetrators coming and crawled under my bunk snug as a bug. Scott, our cabin leader, could never figure out how the other cabin had figured out that it had been us who raided them. Scott, you see, was not very bright, which may well explain why he was still going to 4-H camp at the age of twenty-three.

On the final day of our stay, I awoke from my hour-long power nap (which took place every morning during the rest of the camp's breakfast) and was excited about the events scheduled for that day. Today was "Craft Day" for me, and I was finally going to be able to fulfill my long awaited destiny as the premier soap carver of my time. I quickly rubbed the sleep from my well bloodshot eyes, grabbed my canvas, a bar of Ivory soap, and headed for the craft building. In my haste, I forgot my package of dye and my plain white T-Shirt, which was slated for tie-dying. I spun on my heel and raced back to the cabin to retrieve the overlooked items.

Upon arrival, we were greeted with a neat display of the other campers' soap carvings and an array of some of the more elaborate and colorful tie-dye projects. I remember thinking that some of these folks were obviously professionals at these crafts, as the designs and details were truly awe-inspiring. We were given a brief overview of suggestions for design, as well as an equally brief instruction on how tie-dying was accomplished. As was my custom at the time, I paid very little attention to either of these things and instead daydreamed about the kudos that I was sure to receive when my soap masterpiece finally took shape in physical form as it had appeared in my mind for all this time leading up to today. The counselor had scarcely said the words I had awaited, "Begin your projects," and I was whittling away at my bar of Ivory.

The design I had long since decided on was fairly simple. I

was to carve the figure of a Rainbow Trout, its lean body curved to one side, with its delicate mouth slightly agape. From its top lip was to protrude a depiction of a tiny Royal Coachman Fly. I could see this whole thing as I sat looking at my bar of soap, and now I had only to bring it to life. As I whittled and poked at my bar, I soon found that my zeal, my determination, and my overly-vivid imagination may have far outweighed my artistic talent. After roughly a half-hour of creating, I found myself looking at a chunked out bar of Ivory soap, with a "V" carved in one end where my fish's mouth was supposed to be. As I continued to struggle, my hands began to sweat, and before long my fish was a frothy blob in my frustrated hands. As I would attempt to tighten my grip to accommodate my carving, my fish would shoot from my slimy little hands and onto the floor. Soon my little dirt-encrusted bar of Ivory soap more resembled a hedgehog than a fish. It wasn't long after that that I developed a strong distaste of fish and set about designing a hedgehog. Unfortunately, after another half-hour of trying to bring my hedgehog out of his soapy shell, I was left with a disturbingly small, dirt-encrusted blob of nothing. My hands were covered with soap, my lap was covered with soap, and my eyes burned from having small pieces of soap flip into them throughout my hour-long trial by cleaner. My time was running out, my bar was nearly gone, and I had nothing to show for my effort. I sat alone, disillusioned, and in despair. The realization that my artistic talents were in fact practically nil weighed heavily on my nine-year-old psyche. Soon I began digging a hole at one end of my now two and one half-inch bar of soap. I drilled out a rather large, round area, smoothing the edges for lack of any other ideas. As I sat looking at what I'd done, it occurred to me that my little bar was taking the unmistakable (in my sleep-deprived mind) form of an observatory. I whittled down the sides to accentuate the opening, carved a little door where the miniscule little observatory guy would enter, and sat my tiny chiseled bar on the table before me. The counselor walked by behind me, and much to my dismay stopped to admire my handiwork.

"What did you make?" she questioned.

"Well," I stammered, realizing that the counselor standing behind me was Bonnie, the very woman I had decided earlier in the week that I would one day marry, "I was going to make a fish. . . ." I sighed sheepishly.

"A fish?" she said. "It looks like a lookout to me, and a very nice one too."

"Yeah," I said, flushed with pride, "I decided on a lookout instead." I grabbed my tiny masterpiece and dropped it into my pocket, thinking to myself, "Lookout, observatory, same thing."

Having finished with the carving part of my craft day, I moved on to the tie-dye area. I watched the other kids tie elaborate little knots with string, bunching up areas and leaving others in their original form. I found myself silently wishing that I'd paid more attention to the instructions, and I even considered going over and asking Bonnie to refresh me. Realizing that simply speaking to Bonnie would cause me to likely bite my tongue off, however, I decided it was safer to wing it. I grabbed some string, mixed up my red dye, and started tying knots. I had an idea of what design I was going for and truly thought I might actually pull it off. I dipped my shirt, hung it to dry, and waited, silently wondering what I had created. I envisioned a sun with awesome rings around it, shining down on a simple landscape around the hem of my shirt. What I unveiled was a target with a bright red bull's-eye right in my midsection.

"Ironic," I thought as I stared at my surprisingly well laid out target. "I should have been wearing this all week."

As I stood gazing at yet another blow to my artistic aspirations, counselor Bonnie's sweet voice broke the silence. "A bull's-eye," she stated simply "Groovy, little man."

My head must have turned as red as my newly-dyed shirt, and if I'd had one ounce of energy left in my small body, I would no doubt have run screaming from the room. I didn't, however, so I simply turned around grinning and said, "Yeah, it's a bull's-eye shirt."

I never went back to 4-H camp. In fact, I never went to any kind of camp after that at all. Maybe it was the sleep deprivation, or perhaps the food, or lack thereof, in order that I might get even a little sleep during those times when no one was around. Or perhaps it was the realization that I would never be a sculptor—or any kind of artist, for that matter. The reasons, I suppose, don't really matter in the larger scheme of things. I simply decided that I was not cut out for camp life. Much better I decided that I just go through life with the memory of that week in 1969. That and a well-placed target right on my gut.

And do you know that after all these years, I'm glad I went. I'm quite sure that after reading this you would rightfully wonder why. Well, my friends, it's about memories. Good, bad, or indifferent, I love my memories. I have told my kids this story countless times, each time embellishing or highlighting different aspects. It is one of my son Kellen's favorites, as he has always reveled in stories of my misfortune. I have long ago lost my sculpture. My "groovy" target shirt has long since passed. And I obviously never actually married counselor Bonnie. But like the 4-H pledge, I will never forget any of these things as long as I live.

Chapter 16

HORSE WRECKS

My first horse wreck occurred at the tender age of one and a half. That's right, one and a half years old. My pony, Moody, who was still technically my bother's pony at the time, decided to show me what trotting was. Since at the time I lacked the proper motor skills to handle the change of pace, I crashed and sustained my first broken bone. Needless to say, my memory of this event is sketchy at best, but since it involved a broken collarbone, I thought it was worthy of mention.

Actually, through the ages of one through five, I would venture to guess all my wrecks were attributable to horses—aside from the occasional tricycle mishap or that time taking the "box car" down the basement stairs and into the concrete wall.

I remember vividly one wreck that wasn't even mine that stood out as a real hum dinger. That was one that my brother, Rowdy, had on his Shetland pony, Ginger.

Ginger was what one might call a free spirit. She was a great horse, but she had definite ideas about acceptable behavior. As I've mentioned, if she found her rider in violation of this behavior, she had strong convictions about the proper discipline and was well equipped to deliver it. One day, as Rowdy and I were fiddling around in the corral on our horses, we decided that we should try our hand at barrel racing. We set up the barrels in the customary cloverleaf pattern and proceeded to run our trusty steeds through the course. Moody was what I like to call "velocity challenged." His high gear was just slightly above park, and in order to jog his memory of what running was all about, he required some, how shall I say, persuasion. This persuasion came in the form of a fiberglass switch, referred to as a "bat," which was applied liberally to his rear end in an effort to jog his memory, as that was apparently where it resided.

Moody never seemed to mind the bat, but Ginger was another story. Rowdy found that out the hard way on that fateful summer day. As we ran the barrels, Rowdy, who was seldom satisfied with the speed or precision of his team's efforts, got the foolhardy notion that with just a modicum of persuasion, Ginger could set the all time land speed record for barrel racing. I questioned the wisdom of this theory, but as per usual, Rowdy was not to be denied in his quest for greatness. I handed over the bat and retreated to a safe distance. Our corral, I should note, was split into two separate parts, one large pen in which all of the horses resided, and another smaller pen for the ponies to go into to eat. The smaller pen was separated by one large two-by-twelve board that was strategically nailed across the opening at exactly the height of a Shetland pony. This way the big horses couldn't go under and eat all the pony's food.

As Rowdy and Ginger started the cloverleaf pattern, I could tell that Rowdy was eager for more speed. I watched as he brought the bat down on Ginger's backside between the first and second barrel. Ginger tucked her flowing white tail, and I saw her pin her ears. It was obvious to me that my big brother was flirting with disaster. Surely, I thought, he felt the tail tuck and saw the ears pin, which was the universal indication of unacceptable behavior. Apparently not, for as they rounded the last barrel and headed for home, which was the barn and the pony pen, Rowdy let out a whoop and brought the bat down hard on Ginger's rump. Rowdy was nearly ejected instantly as Ginger lurched into warp drive, making a beeline for the pony pen. With her ears pinned tightly to her head, it was evident that some insolent child was going to pay dearly for his transgressions. Rowdy's eyes were the size of dinner plates as his mount rocketed toward the waiting two-by-twelve that was sure to brush him into oblivion. Mom happened to be coming out to the barn at the point of terminal velocity. "Jump!" I yelled, thinking it far better to bail and deal with the ground than take one's chances with "The Board of Death."

Rowdy, apparently seeing Mom through his tear-filled eyes, began wailing at the top of his lungs, "I didn't hit her with the bat! I didn't hit her with the bat!"

"Jump, you idiot!" I yelled again, but apparently Rowdy either didn't hear my sound advice or, as was more likely, he simply chose not to adhere to it.

What happened next was both remarkable and horrifying. At the exact time Ginger reached the board, it seemed she had a change of heart and decided that death was too strong a price for her rider to pay, even though it was probably deserved, and she jumped. She jumped up, planting the two-by-twelve firmly on her airborne chest. The cracking of the board, the screeching of the nails, and the terrified yell of an eight-year-old boy rang through the summer air. To Rowdy's credit, he was able to hang on as Ginger smashed through the board and into the pony pen. Sadly, Ginger was not about to let him off scot-free, and she proceeded to pile drive him with her patented "sunfish" maneuver, leaving him a wriggling mass of dried horse waste.

I sat on Moody, stunned and amazed at what had just occurred. Mom was making her way to her wounded offspring, and Ginger was over it all and enjoying the leftovers from last night's grain.

Rowdy survived the great "bat attack" somehow and, aside from a few bumps, bruises, and occasional sliver, was none the worse for wear. As Mom walked with him toward the house, presumably to pick stickers, she handed me my fiberglass bat. "Did he hit her with this thing?" she asked me.

"I—I, don't think so, Mom," I said. "Ginger's just crazy, you know."

"Well," Mom said, "I know somebody in this horse pen is...."

And that's all that was said about it. That was a classis horse wreck.

You know, now that I think about it, I can't remember a time when any other horse besides Ginger ever bucked me off. Many have tried, but somehow I was always able to weather the storm. Maybe it was because I was younger then, or maybe it was because we did far more stupid things on our ponies than we ever did on regular-size horses. I'm not sure the reason, but of this I am sure. That pony could buck. If she wanted you off, she would get you off, period, end of story.

I remember one day, Rowdy and I were getting ready to go riding in the woods behind my grandparents' house. Rowdy was going to ride Spud, his horse at the time, and I was going to take Ginger. As I saddled up that morning, I could tell that my mount was not nearly as enthused about going on this outing as I was. She was hard to catch. She crowded me into the wall of the barn as I tried to put her saddle on, and she blew herself up like a puffer fish when I tried to cinch her up. I had known her long enough to realize that all was not well in Gingerville.

Regardless, I was determined to make her comply with my wishes. Mistake number one. I led her out of the barn and into the corral to wait for Rowdy, who was not quite ready. As I climbed onto Ginger's back, I felt her stiffen beneath me. Since it had been a long time since she had bucked me off, I shrugged it off and decided to take a lap or two around the pen. She had scarcely made three steps before she came completely uncorked. Since I was paying no attention, I didn't stand a chance and found myself flat on my back, fighting for oxygen. Slowly air once again filled my lungs, and I was on my way to catch my renegade horse.

"This time," I thought to myself, "I'll be ready." I gathered her up and climbed back aboard. Again, she stiffened. I tried to reason with her, stroking her neck and talking softly to her. Once again we set off around the pen, and once again I found myself being pounded off the dirt. This time, when I regained my composure, not to mention my breath, I simply sat up, wondering what to do. I knew that I had no choice but to get back on, but I also knew that I had little or no chance of riding her if she wanted to buck me off. Rowdy and Spud came out of the barn as I sat there, covered in dirt, my head reeling. Rowdy came over and asked what had happened. I told him the whole sordid story and how I was sure that when I got back on I was just going to get plunked again. I tried to convince him to take a crack at her, but since she had been his horse for years, he was not biting. As I sat, pondering my predicament and dreading what I knew had to be done, Ginger walked over to the spot where I sat. I may have said something soft and soothing to her, but more likely I told her in no uncertain terms what a sway-back, knock-kneed fleabag she was. Anyhow, she seemed to understand and nudged me with her muzzle.

"Sure," I said, "you just want to buck me off again." I

pushed her hard away, mumbling about my misfortune of having the most worthless horse in the known world. Back she came, bumping me with her nose. "Okay," I said, "let's get this over with." I climbed back aboard.

I don't know what it was with her that day, and why she felt the need to put me in my place, but it seemed she was over it. Much to my relief, she didn't buck me off again. Nor to my memory did she ever try again. I loved that dumb pony.

Fortunately for Rowdy and me, horse wrecks to be remembered were not limited to us. My cousin, Tom, for instance, had one of the most memorable wrecks ever, and he hardly ever even rode. Tom was a great cousin to grow up with, as his sense of humor complemented his rather lumpy stature and his flaming red hair. He was a riot. He was, however, not a horseman. The only time I can recall riding with him was on a saddle club trip to Boulder Creek, high in the mountains surrounding our home of Bonners Ferry, Idaho. Tom had a little Pinto pony at the time, and I can't remember if it even had a name. That was just the way cousin Tom was. He never got in a hurry to do anything, including naming his pets.

Tom and his mystery pony, Rowdy and Ginger, and me and Moody set off that morning to do a little scouting along the creek for prospective fishing holes. The rest of the grownups were getting ready for the trail ride that was scheduled for later that afternoon as we set off on our own. We had ridden for a half-hour or so, and the fog was beginning to lift off the meadow of which the creek was nestled. We talked and laughed as Tom struggled to stay aboard his steed. He was finally starting to get the hang of it when we came to a place where we could go no farther without crossing the shallow water of Boulder Creek. Rowdy and I led the way down the bank, onto the sandy shore, and across the six-foot wide stream of bubbling water. We never considered there might be a problem until we heard

Tom shouting obscenities behind us. Seems Tom's horse had an aversion to water that we had not heard about.

"C'mon," I shouted, "get that jug head over here." Tom smiled amiably at my perceived impatience and stuck his hands out to his sides as if to ask for an explanation of just how I expected him to accomplish this feat.

"Turn her around, go back up the bank, and get a run at it," Rowdy explained. "She won't even know what's going on till she's through the creek." I nodded agreement and watched as Tom turned the horse around and headed up the bank. He retreated probably twenty yards, grabbed the saddle horn, and put the boots to his balking pony. The pony took off toward the creek as Tom scratched and clawed to stay atop her galloping frame. Down the bank and to the stream's edge, she came like shot from a gun. Sadly, for poor Tom, the stream's edge was as far as this horse had in mind to go. She locked up the brakes, ducking her head and planting her hooves into the sandy creek bed. Tom was obviously unprepared for this rapid change of pace and was propelled forward at an alarming rate. Since he had a death grip on the saddle horn, and was not of diminutive stature, the saddle slid forward at nearly the same rate as he. Splash! He went head long into the frigid waters of Boulder Creek. He came out of the water, spitting, spewing, and looking much like a wet, red-haired sea creature. His horse would have liked to run away, but since the saddle was lodged on the back of its neck, and the cinch was tight around the backs of its front legs, all it could do was stand, head down, waiting for help from an unlikely source. Since Rowdy and I were always taught to be sympathetic to folks in need, we stopped our hysterical laughter as soon as we possibly could.

Tom stood in the middle of the creek, dripping and shivering from the cold, as we dismounted and set about helping his horse out of its predicament. Tom saw this act as some odd type of betrayal, that our first priority would be to help is stupid horse. He made his way out of the water, a thin stream of sand trickling down his furrowed brow.

"Just get a run at it, huh?" he grumbled. "I could have drowned."

"Yeah," Rowdy agreed as he tightened the cinch on Tom's saddle.

"But you didn't, and man, that was the best wreck that I have ever seen."

"No kidding," I agreed, desperately trying to stifle the chuckles that kept involuntarily emanating from my body. "Your eyes were HUGE! Ha ha, and the splash you made— Sssplooosh! It was a classic. You should be proud, you big dope."

"I suppose you'd like to see me do it again, wouldn't you, wart?" he said, rapidly regaining his stellar sense of humor.

"Oh gosh, would you?" I begged.

Well Tom wouldn't do it again, although he was good enough to do a couple belly flops into the creek as a sort of safe and sane reenactment of the event. As I said, Cousin Tom was awesome to grow up with, and his horse wreck still stands out as the all time greatest.

Chapter 17

PRINCIPLE MATTERS

I would be completely remiss in writing stories about horses without mentioning Pancho Villa. Pancho was the son of my Aunt Kelly's horse, Stormy, and my grandpa's stallion, Dandy Dunbar (or Scooter, as he was known to us).

Scooter was a magnificent animal, possessed of all the fire and grace the good Lord could possibly bestow on a creature. I can remember standing on the fence watching him as he pranced around his pen, eyes wide and alert, nostrils flared, and muscular neck bowed, sending what seemed to be a challenge to any and all that might cross him. He was the only horse I can remember ever being afraid of.

Pancho was blessed with many of his father's features: his head, eyes, and even the way he carried himself. He, too, was a truly beautiful horse. Smaller in stature than his sire, he was classed a P.O.A., or Pony of America, but be assured, he was no pony. I loved him the first time I saw him, and to this very day I get a warm feeling whenever I say his name. That's how much he meant to me. Unfortunately, he was not completely without fault, as things seldom are, and that's where I begin this story.

When we got Pancho, we had moved to a 3,500-acre cattle ranch called the J.N.B. We had finally reached cowboy heaven. Dad was the ranch foreman and, as such, was in charge of watching over the herd. He was a fence fixer, veterinarian, and midwife all rolled into one. Because there were well over a thousand cows to care for, it seemed to be a never-ending task.

I loved to ride along with Dad and do what I could to help out. This usually involved meandering through the cows and calves looking for teary eyes, which was a sign of pink eye, or dirty behinds, which indicated scours, a disease that dehydrates and, if left untreated, kills young calves. I filled many syringes with pink eye medicine and antibiotics and even got to administer many doses myself. I felt very important and considered myself quite the nine-year-old veterinarian.

It was on one of these excursions that Pancho and I encountered our first true battle of wills. As he had a definite mind of his own, we had worked through small glitches before, but nothing quite like this one.

Dad and I had finished working one pen of cows and were on our way to another. In order to save time, Dad decided that instead of going all the way back to the bridge to cross the creek, which stood between our desired destination and us, we would just take the horses through the creek and up the other side. We rode down the bank to a likely crossing point, and Dad and his horse splashed right through. I pointed Pancho toward the water, and he made it perfectly clear that he was in no way interested in saving time.

I felt him tense up and watched his ears flatten to his neck. He whirled around and, in two quick jumps, was back where we had started atop the bank.

I was not at all impressed with his display of rampant insubordination and told him so while his muzzle was pinned to my knee as we made rapid circles. He'd had a fit, I'd had a fit, and I figured we were even. Seems Pancho didn't agree.

I straightened him up, patted him on the neck, and tried to make him understand that the rushing water wasn't going to hurt him. Dad looked on impatiently as we slowly and carefully made our way back down the steep bank.

Again Poncho's muscles tightened as he reached out with his muzzle to try to get a whiff of what this strange, scary obstacle was made of. He inched one step closer, and his front foot slipped across a moss-covered rock and into the water. That was enough of that, and he reared, spinning back toward and up the bank. This time I wasn't as ready, and I shot back off my saddle and onto his rear. Fortunately, I had a death grip on my saddle horn and was able to cling to the fleeing animal. But the ride had taken its toll. I thought I was hurt, the horse and I were both scared, and for one fatal moment, the trip back to the bridge didn't seem so far.

I told my dad what I was thinking. He didn't agree, which I was pretty sure he wouldn't, as now this event had taken on *principle.* Dad has always been a man of exceedingly strong principle. He glowered out from beneath the wide brim of his old felt cowboy hat and said simply, "No, you just wait there." I didn't care for his tone and immediately did what I always did, cried. I don't know why, he would never hurt me, I knew that, but I knew this didn't bode well for my silly horse.

Back across the creek he and his horse came. I'm sure Major, Dad's horse at the time, was just as disgusted as Dad that one of his own kind would show such lack of control.

"What are you bawling at? You hurt?" Dad asked as he rode up beside me.

"I banged my knee when I slid off the saddle," I lied.

"Well, let's get across this creek so we can get to work," he said, as if it were the simplest thing in the world.

"Pancho won't!" I whined. Dad shot me a look that froze the blood in my veins.

"Pancho will!" he hissed and slipped his lariat around my horse's neck.

I urged my horse forward to the creek's edge where again he stopped. This time, however, there would be no turning back. As Dad neared the other bank, the rope came tight and Pancho strained against the pressure. I grabbed the saddle horn and squeezed my knees as tightly as I could, preparing for the storm. Turns out it was a good thing.

Dad's horse had two feet out of the water on the far bank when Pancho decided to make his move. As I said before, he had a mind of his own and had decided privately on a compromise. He'd cross the stupid creek, but no one said he had to get wet. He launched himself skyward and toward the other bank. The g-forces pulled at me as we sailed across the stream below, causing me to slide almost to the back of the saddle till my knees caught the swells. We flew for what seemed like a mile, actually about twelve feet, and came crashing down almost on top of Dad and Major. The radical drop in g-forces flung me forward and ultimately into too close contact with the saddle horn I gripped so tightly. Now I began to cry in earnest.

At first Dad was shocked, then scared, and then mad about the way this simple crossing had transpired. He, too, had a mind of his own and decided that not only would Pancho cross the creek, but he would also get wet.

Back across the creek we headed. Then three more times after that until Pancho realized that the water didn't hurt and wasn't nearly as scary as the nut on the other end of the rope. We ended up almost exactly where we had started, and Dad slipped the noose off the now soaked horse.

He looked at me with the look of a concerned father and asked softly, "Robb, are you all right?"

"Yes," I mumbled, fighting to compose myself and wipe the flood of tears from my mud-speckled face.

"Okay," he said, "let's go to the other side then." And we did just as simple as that.

When we reached the road on the far side, we rode silently for probably fifteen minutes. Then Dad chuckled quietly to himself. My head snapped over, as I couldn't believe what I was hearing. Then a smile broke across his face as he began to laugh and laugh and laugh.

"What is so darned funny?" I asked, sure that he was laughing about what a baby I had been.

He composed himself, smiled, and shook his head. "That was as fine a piece of riding as I have ever seen. I don't know how you hung on, kid."

I beamed with pride and started to laugh as I thought of the look on Dad's face as seven hundred pounds of horseflesh flew across the water right at him. I'm still not sure I actually saw it, as my eyes were probably closed, but somehow this picture popped into my mind. It still does.

Dad and I laughed and joked about that episode all day: Dad doing slow-motion reenactments and me contorting my face to try to match the terrified expression. It was a great day, and now I'm forever grateful to my bonehead horse for acting the fool and teaching me two valuable lessons in the process: the first being that just because something seems scary or hard doesn't mean you don't have to do it, and secondly, if you're going to do something, you might just as well do it willingly and correctly the first time. It saves a lot of headaches in the end. Thanks, Pancho Villa.

Chapter 18
SLEDDING DOS AND DON'TS

During the Christmas season, as the temperature drops and snowflakes cascade from the heavens, my mind is taken back to a memorable pastime of my youth—that being sledding and all the many forms that it takes. There are certainly nearly as many options for vehicles or sliding devices as one's imagination can conjure. Anything from the extraordinarily simple plastic garbage bag to a high-tech, super-slick, scientifically-engineered, quad ski, handle bar, and brake-fitted all titanium Wonder Sled. Equal parts snow, sleds, time, kids, and of course, one incredibly steep hill, preferably with trees or fencing at the bottom, are all ingredients necessary to create the perfect winter recreation, which could also be spelled "wreckreation."

Being an avid sled enthusiast since my dad first strapped my car seat to a toboggan to celebrate my first Christmas, I consider myself somewhat of an expert in the field. As such, I feel it is my moral responsibility to shed some light on the many dos and don'ts involved in this pursuit. So here for you now, and indeed all of prosperity, whatever that is, is the Complete

Guide to Sledding Aptitude. Since I would hate to begin this manual with a negative feel, I shall start with the must dos first.

Do be prepared for changing snow conditions — Nothing is more heartbreaking than to walk all the way to your hill of choice only to find that the snow that you presumed to be puffy, fluffy, and dry is now a wonderful sheet of solid, glowing, rock hard ice, and you without your runner sled, metal saucer, or old car hood. What a tragedy, as you are forced to slide slowly along on your big plastic tub as people scream past you, showering you with their ice roost as they hurtle toward the fence or trees below.

Do be courteous to others — In the likely event that you take a spill and find yourself sprawled half-conscious in the path of oncoming sledders, don't be too quick to jump up and make a dive for safety. This deprives your sledding partners of one of the funnest and most satisfying parts of the sledding experience—that of running over downed riders. Best to simply assume the fetal position, covering your ears, nose, and toes, and allow your friends to run the entire length of your half-frozen body. If you aren't a fan of the fetal method, try this: Simply stand straight up, put your hands high in the air, and scream like a banshee while your buddy clips your feet out from under you, sending you sailing over him and his sled to the track below.

This method saves his momentum, plus allows the person following him to join in the fun.

Do sled at all hours and in all conditions — Nothing is worse in my mind than a picky sledder. Or as some call them, a "Sled 'O'Donna." Just because it's forty below and one wrong move could make your runner sled a lifetime part of your facial features doesn't mean it isn't the perfect time to sled. It's toward the end of the season, it's raining, and one third of the run is mud and rock. Perfect terrain for skidder tubes with fourteen kids piled high. Mud slides too!

All hours of day or night are suitable for sledding. Some of my most memorable trips have taken place on a dark cloudy night when I could barely see my hand in front of my face.

Imagine the excitement of realizing that a barbed wire fence is a mere three feet in front of you while zipping along about forty on an icy path in the pitch dark. Now those are memories you don't soon forget.

Do take your less-experienced friends — Let's say you have a cousin from the city and once a year he comes to visit around Christmas. Take him along. What a wonderful way to show him or her that it's possible to enjoy all the fun and physical benefits that you enjoy every day and night all winter long. In fact, beginners actually are often more fun than experienced sledders, as they tend to fall off more, affording more opportunity for run downs or foot clippers. Also because they are often ill-prepared, one can even score an occasional appendage in the bargain. Finally, most beginners haven't the slightest idea about what lies at the bottom of the average sledding hill, thus affording you a perfect opportunity to hang back and enjoy a head long pile up into a ninety-foot Bull Pine. What fun!

Do take your parents (after Christmas) — Hey, parents need an occasional thrill, too, and what better way to achieve familial closeness than to take Mom to the fence or send Dad sailing head over teakettle into the ice or snow.

Please note, however, the *after* Christmas part. It is important to remember that most parents are somewhat frail, and indeed, in some instances, wimpish. Any bone deep cut, dislocation, or lost appendage is almost always followed by a hospital visit and lost wages. This is bad, as it cuts into the funds that they otherwise may have set aside for Christmas gifts. *Be smart, sledders.*

That should about cover the must do portion, and now in the interest of safety, fair play, and fun, I will touch on just a few of the most very important don't dos.

Don't cry — This is far and away the most important don't of all. There is no crying in sledding for two main reasons. Doing so is a hazard to yourself and other sledders. Just imagine this scenario, if you will. You fall off, and your buddy rightfully runs the entire length of your body. It's forty below, but you start blubbering about the trivial loss of an ear or something. What does crying create? Moisture, of course! So there you are, standing in the middle of the path and spraying water like a Lawn King sprinkler, when along comes another buddy who sees and proceeds to execute a perfect foot clipper. Since your hands are over your ears and not over your head as they should be, the trajectory of your body is compromised, and, thanks to all the tears combined with the forty below temperature, your face is now a permanent part of your friend's rear. Granted, over a period of time you will thaw, but imagine the embarrassment you would have caused your friend in the meantime. No, no, no crying in sledding! Also there is no better way to kill a mood, and it is well documented the adverse effects that tears have on a well-groomed sled run. If for some reason you feel tears coming on, I have found it best to quickly throw yourself into the nearest bush, taking care to poke some foreign object into your eyes to account for the tears streaming down your cheeks. Whatever course of action you decide to take in this regard, it is far superior to allowing your friends to believe that you are actually crying while sledding. There is no crying in sledding!

Don't be a bad sport — If your friend gets a good run going and catches you from behind, it is proper etiquette to raise ones feet over your back, thus allowing him access to your exposed runners so that he may flip you sideways and off the path into the ditch or possibly a tree. This is not a personal assault and should be taken in the good-natured spirit that it is intended. This is all part of the fun, and maybe next time you can catch him or her and pin their feet to the front of the sled so they can't bail at the bottom of the hill and may instead enjoy an up close and personal visit with Mr. Bull Pine. Sportsmanship is very, very important.

Finally, **Don't be a fraidy cat!** — Nobody likes a fraidy cat.

Let's say one of your comrades nabs an old car hood from the local junkyard. He spends all night and part of the next day waxing and polishing his prize. Then he, with a heroic effort, drags the two hundred-pound piece of steel to the tippy top of the steepest hill in the world and invites you and about ten of his closest friends to join him on his maiden voyage. Imagine how heartbroken he would be if after surveying the straight-down, jump-covered, tree-infested sled course, you turn chicken. Even one person's weight could mean the difference between excellence and mediocrity in such a venture, so suck it up and don't *ever* be a fraidy cat.

Well, that should about cover it. By following these few simple rules, you, too, can enjoy a lifelong passion for sledding, like me. Enjoy yourself. Happy sledding. I've got a car hood to wax.

Chapter 19

BEAR SLAYER

Have you ever read a story in one of those outdoor magazines about how a renegade bear turns on its pursuer and becomes the hunter, rather than the hunted, and the horrific scenario this presents? Well, I have, and to go one better, in the spirit of outdoor magazines, here is my own personal version of "This Happened to Me."

It was the fall of my eleventh year on this planet earth, and for all intents and purposes, I had long since passed the threshold from boyhood to man. Standing a whopping four feet six and tilting the scales at a strapping sixty-five pounds, I was sure that anyone who saw me recognized my obvious machismo. As hard as it may be to believe, however, there were doubters amuck who insisted on labeling me as something less. Things like, Kid, Punk, Shrimp, Snot-nosed Little So and So . . . et cetera.

I recognized, of course, that these comments were borne out of jealousy, but still sometimes I felt a twinge of inadequacy because of them. Sometimes I felt I just needed something, some opportunity to show these doubters once and for all the stuff I was really made of. It is said "be careful what you wish for" for a reason.

At the time of this event, we were living on the J.N.B. cattle ranch, some twenty-five miles from our hometown of Bonners Ferry, Idaho. The ranch was nestled at the base of the Westside Mountains, a part of the Selkirk Range, and was home to not only our domestic animals, but a wide variety of wildlife, as well. These included, elk, deer, moose, and, of course, the most fearsome and unpredictable creature of all . . . Mom. Seriously though, the creature I refer to is none other than the magnificent North American Black Bear.

Rowdy, who was an avid reader of outdoor magazines, had told me many tales of marauding bears who stalked the forests in search of eleven-year-old, four-feet-six-inch men to capture, torture, kill, and ultimately consume. Since I detested reading of any type, I never read any of the accounts, but since Rowdy was my older, all-knowing, all-seeing mighty one, I took his word without question and remained diligently on guard at all times.

One morning as Rowdy and I were going about doing our chores of feeding the cattle, we were confronted by a frightening discovery. At the top grain bin, scarcely a quarter mile away from our house, the metal door to the bin had been bent nearly in half. The distinct scratch marks, and well-placed piles of partially-digested wild apples and elderberries, left little question as to what had gone on the previous night. We had been paid a visit by Carnivorous Horriblous, or in laymen's terms, a big flippin' bear. A chill swept through me as I imagined the creature, whom Rowdy estimated at ten feet tall and nearly 1,500 pounds, hooking the edge of the steel door with his razor sharp, sixteen-inch claws and bending it like paper so he could satisfy his insatiable appetite, until he could come up with the much preferred four-feet-six, eleven-year-old man.

"Do you think he got all he wanted and moved on?" I asked, trying to mask my concern by forming actual words rather than the steady rhythmic Duh, Duh, Duh sounds that had been escaping my quivering lips for approximately five minutes.

"Nope, I don't think so," Rowdy said, assuming his very wise stance. "You see, I read in *Outdoor Life* that once a bear finds a source of food, he'll hang around and watch over it, protecting it till it's gone."

"Watch over it?!" I blurted. I'm sure I must have resembled that girl off the movie *The Exorcist* as my head spun round and round, expecting at any moment to see a big black blur flying in my direction, his eyes shooting fire, nostrils flared, and a hideous drool oozing from his cavernous maw. I think Rowdy sensed my growing anxiety because he said, "Don't get all worked up, snot nose. He won't be back till dark."

"Oh, thank God," I murmured to myself. Hey, snot nose?! What in the heck was that all about? My own brother, for crying out loud.

"I'm no snot nose," I hissed as I snatched a bucket of grain and headed for the truck.

It was at precisely that moment that an idea began to take shape. An idea spawned of frustration, fear, and unadulterated male bravado. I knew then what I must do. I had to face my childish fears. I must slay the dragon—er, bear. By killing the bear, I reasoned, I would surely become a hero. No, not simply a hero—a legend. No, better yet, I would become the Great Bear Slayer. The only question that remained was how. I owned a gun, but sadly it seemed that my .22 caliber single shot just would not be adequate firepower for a job of this magnitude. Since bazookas were scarce in our area, I decided the weapon of choice would be Dad's ol' .32 Winchester Special. I also saw that it would be wise to keep my plan under wraps, lest someone else might covet the title of Great Bear Slayer for themselves.

All day long, I planned and plotted. Each detail or possible complication was weighed and analyzed. I even went so far as to draw a detailed diagram as to how the operation would go. It went something like this. Under cloak of darkness I, Bear Slayer, would sneak down the road, bearing only the ol' .32, a five-pound flashlight, and all the courage my manly frame could muster. I would have to sneak in total darkness as I approached my quarry from the rear. When I reached the "Red Zone," or the area that I had designated to take my first shot, I would simply click on the light, confusing and quite possibly blinding my target, raise my trusty weapon, and place a 150 grain bullet between his glowing eyes. I then figured to do the obligatory dance of joy, and then go get my brothers and neighbors so they could see what an incredibly manly man I was.

Things really started to fall into place as the day rolled on. My parents were going to town for their weekly square dancing session, and Rowdy was going over to Larry's house, presumably to discuss new ideas for torturing Larry's little brother, Jaffry, and me. This left me and my little brother, Ron, home alone.

Initially, I did see Ron as an encumbrance to my well laid out plan; however, there were two details that continued to nag at me. Number one was that because the ol' .32 being nearly my height, and only slightly less than half of my weight, it was going to require my full attention come the moment of truth. That left the five-pound, fifty-thousand candlepower flashlight unaccounted for. This, I decided, was a perfect job for Brother Ron. Since his five-year-old stature was such that he was the perfect height to stand behind me as I knelt down, he could flip on the light and be witness to his big brother's crowning moment. The other thing that concerned me was that as conscientious, responsible adult, I could not possibly leave a small child unattended. Far better that he goes with me, I reasoned. I assure you that this plan had nothing to do with what others perceived as my intense fear of the dark, as I can truthfully say that I am not, nor have I ever been, afraid of the dark—simply the creatures that lurked about in it. With these final two hurdles cleared, all that remained was to wait.

Minutes turned to hours, and soon it was time for Mom and Dad to go. We said our goodbyes and, of course, Mom gave her ever present commands: be good; watch your brother; don't stay up too late; and . . .

"Robb, why are you pushing me out the door?"

"No reason, Mom. I just hate to see you late for square dancing," I lied as convincingly as possible.

Finally the car's taillights were safely out of sight, Rowdy was gone to Larry's, and all systems were go for operation Bear Slayer. As I scurried around, gathering up the necessary equipment, Ron watched with quiet interest. I told him to get his coat and boots on and gave a brief rundown of the events that were about to take place and what his role was to be in them.

When I had finished my briefing, he simply blinked his oversized brown eyes and said, "Nope, I don't wanna."

Fortunately I had considered this very possibility and was able to sway him with an offer he could never refuse. "I'll be your best friend."

"Okay," he said happily and trotted off dutifully to retrieve his coat and boots.

Butterflies the size of B-52s clamored around in my stomach as we stepped into the darkness of the moonless light. I found little comfort in Ron's non-stop chatter as we moved slowly down the road toward the granary. At the top of the hill, we stopped, and I once again went over Ron's responsibilities with him, knowing all too well that timing was everything if we were to maintain the element of surprise. It was a mere five hundred yards from the place we now stood to the grain bin and ultimate glory. I emphasized the importance of absolute silence to Ron by explaining the distinct possibility of death by consumption by our intended target, and it seemed to work, as it may well have been the only time I can remember Ron being quiet for more than five minutes.

As we neared the "Red Zone," it became painfully apparent that any subconscious hopes I may have harbored that our intended quarry might turn out to be a no-show faded as we could now clearly hear the unmistakable sound of claws scratching steel and the distinct sound of a great weight slamming against the granary door. My heart raced wildly. I could see only roughly ten feet in front of me, and it began to occur to me that my master plan had more flaws than previously supposed. Finally we reached the shooting area, and I knelt down trying to steady my tattered nerves, as well as Dad's gun. Slam, slam, slam went the door as the beast was apparently totally oblivious to our presence.

"Ready?" I whispered.

"Yep," was Ron's reply as he flipped the switch on the Megalight.

The events that followed remain somewhat confused, even after all these years, but there are some things that I recall with distinct clarity. One is the sight of a bear, standing no less than twenty feet tall and a minimum of fifteen feet wide, perfectly silhouetted against the shining backdrop of the grain bin. His piggish eyes glowed red as he swung his massive head around to see what insolent boob would dare to invade his domain. Another thing I remember clearly is the eerie deafening shriek that followed this act, flowing like a raging river across my trembling lips, and indeed only a somewhat smaller version emanating from over my shoulder from a body much too small to create such a noise.

The bear, apparently getting a good look at my physique, as well as my fluttering tonsils, and perhaps not relishing the thought of becoming both deaf and blind, let out a bark and disappeared into the darkness. I never fired a shot. It seems I was afflicted with a strange sort of temporary paralysis and was unable to move a muscle.

As the bear slipped out of the intense light beam and into the blackness of night, so also did my visions of becoming The Great Bear Slayer.

My disappointment about this fact was thankfully overwhelmed by another even stronger emotion at that point, however, as I found myself alone, except for Ron, who really wasn't much comfort in the abysmal darkness. To complicate this already terrifying scenario, I had the knowledge that a very large, quite possibly somewhat irritated, grain bin door bending, wild apple and elderberry pile leaving, four feet six, sixty-five pound, eleven-year-old man eating, twenty-seven foot tall, three thousand pound North American Black-hearted Devil Bear stood waiting to pounce. I reasoned I had three viable options. The first of which was to turn the ol' .32 on myself and save the bear the trouble of actually killing me, and possibly saving myself the agony of capture and torture. Number two seemed much more appealing, however somewhat less dignified, as it involved knocking Ron in the head and hoping to distract my tormenter with a morsel of veal à la human. The third was not overly dignified, but it did seem to be the best choice. That was to scream like a little girl and beat feet to the house.

As I wheeled, wailing like a skirt-wearing, pigtail-bearing micro female, I only paused momentarily as I stumbled over

Ron, who obviously didn't have a true grasp of the desperation of our situation or was not yet old and wise enough to interpret the proper course of action.

I have to hand it to the little fella. He caught on quickly, as within about twenty yards I heard coming behind me the distinct sound of the pounding feet of a small boy carrying a large flashlight. I must have been slowed tremendously by the extreme weight of my weapon, as within a few seconds Ron caught and overtook me like a Ferrari would a Greyhound bus.

Amazingly, we made it home alive. That was the upside. Sadly, I was not able to slay the bear, thus forfeiting my claim to the coveted title I had so hoped for. However, with a few well-placed bribes and a modicum of threats, I was able to persuade Ron to never speak of the events of the evening, so I was able to maintain my stature of a MANLY MAN among most of my peers.

The bear, well, he disappeared. It seems he must have tired of the taste of grain, or perhaps, and I consider this more likely, he had seen enough of us and felt all too fortunate to have escaped The Great Bear Slayer.

Chapter 20

BACKPACKING DONE RIGHT

Back in the early seventies, Rowdy and I were drawn into an outdoor activity for which we had been unknowingly in training for many years. This activity was backpacking. Backpacking became all the rage seemingly overnight as it became en vogue to "get back to nature." Fortunately for us it was indeed a very short trip back, as in fact by this time in our lives we had never really left it.

Rowdy was a born leader. He was a trend seeker, an organizer of "Great Adventures," so this new fad was something he embraced with vigor. It wasn't long before he had us both outfitted with packs and an abundance of gear suitable for survival in the wilds of North Idaho.

In the beginning, as I recall, we made several day trips up to various creeks and lakes in our area, spending a night fishing and communing with nature. This was great as far as I was concerned, but sadly it seemed I lacked Rowdy's extensive knowledge as to how a pack trip was "supposed to be." A real pack trip, it seems, lasts no less than a week, and the meals of beans and weenies we had been enjoying around our campfires would be shunned and scoffed at by "true packers." Since I was never one who dealt well with scoffing—or shunning either, for that matter—I was all for moving up into the ranks of "Real Packers."

Hearing this, in fact most likely expecting this, Rowdy set about educating us on the finer points of backpacking. Also, as a sort of graduation, he began planning a grand trip to an obscure mountain lake tucked away high in the Selkirk Mountains called Big Fisher. Mostly I just sat back and watched and listened as Rowdy (as he did with all great adventures) worked tirelessly, some might even go so far as to say obsessively, to see that every minute detail was gone over with a fine-toothed comb. This process took what I would estimate to be a month.

One afternoon, as he sat furiously writing lists, calculating weights, load ratios, weather variables, and every other "able" imaginable, he violently crumpled his last piece of paper and flung it into the garbage.

"We can't do this!" he said disgustedly as he reached into the trash, pulling the crumpled list out, smoothing it, and continuing to gaze at the vast array of numbers scratched upon it. I, too, examined the tattered paper and figures intently, although honestly, I had not the foggiest idea what I was looking for or at.

"Hmmm," I said, scratching my chin, trying to break the ice and possibly spark one of my brother's patented "Great Ideas." As usual, it didn't take very long.

"We just need a third person," Rowdy explained. "But whom?"

"Cousin Tom would go," I volunteered.

"Cousin Tom wouldn't pack a tooth brush if you broke it in thirds," Rowdy said, obviously disgusted at my oversight. This was probably in fact the truth, as it seems Tom was afflicted since birth with a little known disease called, "Lazius Butticus," for which there is no known cure.

"Maybe Dad would want to go," I offered foolishly.

"Dad is allergic to hiking, dummy," Rowdy reminded me.

"The one to take," he said, assuming his very wise stance, "is Mom."

"Mom?" I asked in astonishment. "She's a, well, you know, she's a GIRL!"

"So what?" Rowdy admonished. "She's ten times tougher than you, she can cook, and I'll bet for a chance to get away from Ron's incessant blabbing for a week she'd do it.

Turns out, as he normally was, Rowdy was right on target, and Mom agreed to go without so much as a moment's hesitation. As soon as Mom had confirmed her attendance, Rowdy once again set about planning, plotting, and puzzling over detail after detail, till finally he possessed a comprehensive list of necessary supplies with their weights, measurements, costs, and manufacturers' home phone numbers. So accurate and concise was this list that I believe it was requested by the Smithsonian Institute to be displayed as the "Mother of All Lists."

After its completion, we three packers loaded up the truck and moved to Beverly, Hills that is . . . oops, wrong story. Actually, we loaded up and headed for Spokane, Washington that is. The home of the Outdoor Sportsman, a veritable Mecca of freeze dried foods, lightweight utensils, and all matter of packing necessities. We spent half a year's salary and finally were ready for our much-anticipated trip.

The morning of our departure turned off sunny and bright. After a stick to your rib-ish breakfast of Mom's world-renowned specialty, rice and raisins, we placed our supply-laden packs into the back of "Old Gert," the family truck, and we were gone.

On the way up the mountain, we discussed the week to come, each of us with our own personal vision of what the future held. Personally, my vision was somewhat skewed, as I pictured a relatively short and simple hike of approximately five miles from the trail head to Big Fisher. A family friend, who worked for the forest service, had assured us that the entire trip should take approximately three hours from start to finish. After this cruise into the lake, I was certain there would be ample time to catch a couple dozen of the native cutthroat that resided in the lake by which we planned to make our home for the week.

Unfortunately for my vision, and consequently my feet and back, our old friend from the forest service was one of two things: a black-hearted, sadistic mad man or a complete idiot in the field of judging distance and time. My guess is that he was indeed equal parts of both, as the trail turned out to be no less than ten miles, straight up, with an array of rock and root stair steps to the sky. My pack, having started off weighing in at forty-five pounds, roughly three quarters of my body weight, gained weight at an incredible rate as we climbed. Turns out it is a little known fact that backpacks are designed to double their weight every five miles. A factor Rowdy had obviously misjudged. Though I scarfed Apollo Space Food Sticks at an alarming rate, it did little to relieve the steadily increasing weight of my burden.

Somehow, after a multitude of near death experiences, we leveled out onto a plateau. It was beautiful. The Bear Grass and the Alpine Spruce gave off a scent of pure wildness. The sun, which had graced us all day, balanced precariously on the ridge tops behind us, preparing for its decent into night as we made our way forward on the now flat trail.

"Finally," I muttered to myself, "but where the heck is the

lake?"

Nobody said a word as we made our way forward, all of us, I'm sure, fearing the same thing. This was the *right* trail, wasn't it?

I, being me, could only control my wagging tongue for approximately ten yards.

"Oh my gosh!" I moaned. "There is no lake here! We just climbed twenty miles, and there is no stinking lake! What kind of sadistic idiot would send someone on a wild goose chase like this?! Oh woe is me! Woe is me!"

Mom and Rowdy remained silent and steadfast in their trek, and just as I was about to open up with another barrage of negativity, we saw the lake. About a mile from where we now stood, surrounded by the cliff we stood upon on one side and by a lush green meadow and forest on the other, laid the most beautiful lake I had, or have, ever seen. Much like I understand childbirth is, my agony disappeared, and in its place was an incredible euphoria. The mile to the lake's edge was covered in a scant fifteen minutes, as all of us found energy reserves we thought had long since been depleted.

We set up camp just as Rowdy had diagramed out of his Foxfire survival book, and as Rowdy and I set off to catch our dinner, Mom settled back to enjoy some much deserved R&R.

The fish were fat and plentiful, the weather was fair and warm, and as it turned out, the trip was all that any of us could have dreamed. As we made our way out at the end of that magnificent week, enjoying a new found closeness, we could have never have known that this would be the last such trip we three would ever take together. All we knew was that it had been great and undoubtedly one of the most unforgettable times of our lives.

Chapter 21
CRICK FISHIN'

Over my forty-eight years of life, it seems to me that I have compiled quite a bit of information that I deem valuable in one way or another. In order to pass this on to future generations of unique (spelled useless) information seekers, it occurs to me that perhaps I should jot down some of the most sought after (again spelled useless) tidbits.

Take for instance crick fishin'. This is an area in which over my many years of pursuit, I have achieved an overabundance of knowledge. In order to relieve some of the pressure off my now overcrowded brain, here now is "The Rudimentary Guide to Crick Fishin'"

I believe it was Grandpa Wallace who actually introduced me to crick fishin' and indeed is responsible for teaching me much of what I now know in that regard. Grandma and he used to take Rowdy and me, along with my aunts, Sandy and Kelly, camping up Smith Crick in the Selkirk Wilderness. This, I might add, was long before our government leaders, in all their wisdom, saw fit to import a healthy population of

Grizzlies into that area. Grizzlies' diet, as you may or may not know, consists largely of bugs, berries, and crick fishers. My views on that, however, are fodder for an entirely different story, and I digress.

First of all, for the aspiring crick fisher, I believe that it is important to be familiar with the terms of the sport and how they are to be properly used. Let's start with the most basic and work up.

FISH — Pronounced "fish," not "feesh," like my grandma used to say, strictly to torment us boys. Sadly, both Kelly and Sandy picked up this most annoying habit, and I'm sure this had a lot to do with their eventual banishment from our ventures.

CREEK — Pronounced "crick" not "creeek," again as my incorrigible grandmother did, further spoiling my poor gullible aunts.

FISHING ROD — Pronounced "pole." No true crick fisher would be caught dead telling his partner that he had recently purchased a new fishing "rod." He would instead more appropriately say, "Got me a new pole, Cleatus," or whatever his partner's name may be.

BAIT — Pronounced "worm" or possibly "corn." A lot of would-be crick fishers slip on this one, so don't be fooled. If some derby wearin' greenhorn comes up to you and says, "Hey pard, let's go to the crick and catch some fish," and you wonder about his true credentials as a crick fisher, just ask him, "What'll we catch 'em with?" When his answer is "Oh, I'll bring suitable bait," you've got him. Scoff, snort, and walk away. He's a cheap imposter.

CATCH — Pronounced "ketch." Sometimes I wonder whose idea it was to bring Grandma along in the first place.

WADERS — Pronounced "Pants," "shorts," or "canvas tennies with the toes cut out." If ever while crick fishin' you might encounter some poor misguided soul wearing actual rubber waders, like they try to hawk at sporting goods stores, it is your duty to heckle, laugh, make jokes about, and, yes, in extreme cases, throw rocks at the perpetrator. How else are they to learn of the absolute inappropriateness of their attire? There have been times when Rowdy, Cousin Tom, and I have actually come upon a wader-wearing wannabe who heard us coming and quickly shed his waders, knowing the penalty he would face. This silly person didn't realize that all it took was one look to see that his legs lacked the particular blue hue that a true crick fisher's legs bear after wading a day in sub zero water. This is definitely an instance where rock throwing is appropriate and, in fact, required.

CREEL — Pronounced "forked stick." No true crick fisher would consider strapping something around their neck, lest they end their pitiful lives swinging from a low hanging branch over the "ultimate fishin' hole."

This leads to our final term, which is a little tricky.

COLLAPSABLE POLE — This can be pronounced several different ways: "broken," "busted," "stepped on," "bent over," or finally, a genuine "Popeil Pocket Fisherman." (Any of these is acceptable.)

That should about cover the most commonly misunderstood pronunciations. Now let's move on to some of the more advanced terms and things to watch out for as you embark on your crick fishin' trip.

LUNKER — This is any fish over eight inches, although a seven incher can be construed a lunker in some instances, including a particularly slow day or when caught with a genuine Popeil Pocket Fishermen.

BEAR TRAP — This is an area in a crick bed were the rocks on the bottom are particularly slick and nasty, usually round, and when you step on them they slide apart just enough to slip your foot sideways into the gap created, wedging your foot like a cork in a bottle, nearly breaking your ankle and normally sending you careening either headfirst or tail first into the chilly water. It is customary in such cases to stand up cursing and say something like "blankety blank bear traps!" to warn your fishing partners, and this also gives them the chance to see you drenched and miserable, thus affording them their deserved belly laugh at your expense.

SssssssssssNAKE — This is pretty self-explanatory. However, sometimes with the noise created by rushing water, or distance from the crier, you may only hear "NAKE!" and be confused. However, look to your partner for other telltale signs, such as walking on top of the water or beating wildly at the bank with his new pole or even retreating so fast that he hits a double bear trap and jerks his feet clean off getting free. These are all sure indications that there are snakes about and that the area is to be avoided at all costs. I should add, and this is extremely important, never, ever, ever is belly laughter appropriate in the case of snake sighting. There is *nothing* funny about snakes.

These are a few important terms, but a true professional crick fisher must recognize more than just verbal communication. Body language can speak volumes, as well.

THE FACE FIRST FLOP AND FLOAT — You're second in a line of a three-fisher team, keeping your customary twenty-five-yard spacing, when suddenly Cousin Tom, the lead fisher, flops face first into the crick. Now he doesn't spring right up cursing, so you know he didn't hit a bear trap. Heart attack, you might guess? No, in this case, this was Cousin Tom's reaction to most any stump along the bank that vaguely resembled a bear. **The Face First Flop and Float** for safety was, of course, Rowdy's and my cue to run as fast as we could, roaring our very best bear roar, toward Tom's floating corpse in an effort to scare him senseless, thus chastising him properly for floating through perfectly good fishing holes for no good reason. I can only imagine what any stump that might actually have *been* a bear might have thought of these shenanigans.

SNEAKY PEEKING — This is a dead giveaway to a "fish hoarder." Nothing is lower than a fish hoarder as far as I am concerned, so I am always on the lookout for a **Sneaky Peeker**. Here's what to look for.

A person who spends an inordinate amount of time at a good looking fishin' hole and continually casts quick glances around to see if anyone is taking note of all the **Lunkers** he is pulling out of the hole. Any good crick fisher knows there is a strict three-fish limit or two-Lunker limit per hole when a fishin' party of two or more is in progress. A **Sneaky Peeker** tries to circumvent this rule by not letting on to his partners that he is indeed swarmed by **Lunkers**. Alas, his peeking always gives him away. Severe chastisement and sometimes "fish bombing," which is throwing a car-sized boulder into his fishin' hole, is called for in this instance.

Finally, but certainly not least importantly, watch for the HAND TO MOUTH move. This motion is almost always indicative of your partner sneaking M&M's, or some other fishin' delicacy, on the sly. This is exceptionally rude—and even downright dangerous in cases of extreme hunger and ill temper.

By studying this guide and striving to obey the rules set before you, I believe we can all make crick fishin' enjoyable and safe for all. So go ahead, grab yer pole, go up to the crick, and ketch some fish.

Not you, Grandma. You stay home and STUDY.

Chapter 22

FUN WITH EXPLOSIVES

As the warm summer breezes waft through the big Montana sky, it brings to my mind the approach of another holiday. I have always been a lover of holidays. Christmas, Thanksgiving, and St. Patty's day are all great. However, my single favorite holiday has got to be the Fourth of July. No other holiday is as eagerly anticipated, by me at least, as this day in July. The reasons for this are varied. Obviously, it comes at a great time of the year. The weather is hot, the lake is warm, and it is an ideal time to float around in the family boat, the *SS Nappy Time*. There is also a lot of eating done on the fourth. What with the barbecues, picnics, and yummy summer time snacks like homemade ice cream, this holiday can compete with any other in the food department.

If I were asked to point out one single segment of this holiday that makes it any more worthy of my adoration than any other, however, I could do it in one word: explosives. Most holidays, it seems, revolve around various themes. Christmas, of course, revolves around the birth of Christ or Santa Claus, depending on your faith of choice. Thanksgiving centers on the Pilgrims, or nowadays the kickoff of the Christmas shopping season. And St. Patty's day revolves around leprechauns and green beer. The Fourth of July, though, is all about explosives. Lots of them. This makes the Fourth of July a holiday I can definitely get behind.

From the time I was a little kid, I have been fascinated by fireworks. From the very first time my big brother suckered me into throwing my first aerosol can into the burn barrel, I've been hooked on the big boom. For any of you who might be getting nervous about now, and may even be feeling compelled to call your local FBI agency, relax. I'm not some psycho Unabomber sort by a long shot. The only things I have ever hurt in my pursuit of entertainment by "Boom" is a half dozen snakes, a couple of frogs, and of course, me. Although I harbor absolutely no remorse regarding the snakes (other than the fact there wasn't more), I do feel bad about the frogs. As for myself, I get what I deserve.

When I was little, my brother and I used to save up any money we could find, beg for, or borrow in anticipation of the local fireworks stand's opening. Back in those days, a person could buy many things that are no longer available to the general public. This was a day, after all, when folks were expected to take responsibility for their own actions, and consequently, fingers. Cherry Bombs, M-80s, and the real version of Black Cat firecrackers were always some of the best. Since my brother and I were never very good at being responsible for our own fingers, our parents would not allow us to buy anything they deemed as "too awfully powerful." For this reason, we were invariably forced to seek out our supply of heavy artillery from friends, most of whom were other kids who traveled with the rodeo circuit. Rodeo kids were always a great source of contraband, as just like us they were normally subject to a limited amount of parental supervision and were afforded several ways to make money. Since my brother and I operated a scouting service for the rodeo riders, we were able to secure a pretty decent base of capital for the purchase of fireworks.

The actual purchase of fireworks was a very involved process. The first order of business was, of course, to count up our funds, then shop the various stands to locate the best deals on the items we deemed necessary. The deeming of necessity was normally a long, drawn-out process. My brother, it seemed, always had a skewed concept of what was actually necessary, in my opinion, and more than one battle could be traced back to this process. Since he was older, craftier, and possessed a ruthless right hook, my views in regard to what was required was normally altered considerably by the time these "negotiations" were completed. Once this process was completed, and I had wiped the tears from my cheeks, acquisition was begun in earnest.

Black Cats were a mainstay in our explosive arsenal, as their versatility and destructive nature were unanimously coveted. Bottle rockets were also needed, if only as a self-defense tool against the other kids from the rodeos. Many was the time we were faced with an all out missile attack while sitting around our campsite any time during the first week of July. These battles would go on sometimes for hours, but would normally come to a violent end when the parents of one or both combatants happened carelessly into one of the "red zones." This was always very traumatic, as at this time it was normally determined that we were not actually responsible enough to be in possession of fireworks of any kind and were required to turn over our entire remaining arsenal. This, it seems, was the very reason that my brother always insisted on buying at least a couple packages of "sparklers." I was always against this purchase, and more than once I was rewarded for my arguments in that regard with a well-placed right hook. Rowdy, being two years my senior, possessed considerably more wisdom and forethought than I and took into consideration the possibility of one of these forfeitures. When the time came that one of the neighbor kids dropped a flaming bottle rocket down the back of Dad's shirt, we would dutifully march to the camper and hand over our packages of sparklers and roughly one percent of our stash of bottle rockets. This always seemed to satisfy the folks' desire to remove our store of explosives, while not adversely affecting our ability to defend ourselves or our camp.

As time passed and our days of traveling to rodeos every weekend of the summer came to an end, our love for fireworks changed, but did not wane. Although it was harder to acquire funding for the purchase of an adequate arsenal, somehow we always seemed to be able to come up with a good supply. By this time we were considerably older, though not appreciably wiser, and had discovered the wonders of combining fireworks in an effort to maximize their destructive capabilities. Bundles of Black Cats were taped together and bottle rockets were attached to arrows in order to have the ability for them to travel the necessary distance to land in our neighbor kids' yards. Although this method of warfare provided us with hours of fun, and several memorable scars, it was discontinued because of a minor miscalculation by the neighbor kid, Larry.

Larry was several years older than Rowdy and me and was born with a mean streak unlike any I had ever experienced. One night during the week of the fourth, we were waging a war between his yard and ours. We fired Black Cat-laden arrows back and forth through the night darkness. This was a rare opportunity for us, as normally our parents would have seen one of the streaking explosives and put a kybosh to our battle, but on this particular night our parents were not at home. Rowdy and I maintained our position behind the big pine tree in our yard as we retrieved the arrows that had been shot in our direction, had detonated, and lay harmless in our grass. We would then re-arm them, wait for an opportune moment, then let them fly back in the direction from whence they came. As it seems these things always do, the battle continued to escalate as it went on. Soon an arrow that had sported a bundle of three Black Cats was adorned with no fewer than six. It wasn't long till those six became twelve, and before you knew it, we were being forced to creep closer and closer to our rival's yard in order to reach it with our overweight arrows. During a retreat from one such creep attack, Rowdy kept a wary eye behind us as we rapidly made our way to the safety of the big pine. We were within probably fifteen feet of safety when Rowdy let out a blood-curdling cry of "INCOMING!" At this point we both hit the deck while keeping an eye on the flaming projectile headed in our direction. It arched through the night sky, wobbling slightly as its flight was compromised by the disturbingly large explosive device attached to its end. An almost simultaneous expression slipped from Rowdy's and my lips, "What the heck is *that*?" As we stared in horror, we noticed that the flaming appendage to the incoming arrow greatly resembled what we immediately recognized as an M-80. An M-80, I should point out, is the fireworks version of a nuclear bomb, and it was often rumored to have the power of a quarter stick of dynamite. The fact that Larry was breaking out the nukes struck fear to the deepest parts of our young souls.

As we watched in horror, the M-80-bearing arrow sailed over our ducked and covered heads and continued its flight until it made contact with the base of the door of our house. Roughly two seconds after contact, it exploded, sending shrapnel flying in all directions. When the pieces stopped raining down around us, Rowdy and I walked slowly forward to survey the damage. A shredded welcome mat, the distinct stench of spent sulfur, and a six-inch hole in the base of our front door stood testament to the nuclear attack we had been subjected to. Fearing a follow up, we quickly gave the sign for surrender by turning our ultra high-powered flashlights on and making an X in the sky with their beams. We could hear the cheering from the neighbor's yard as they recognized this sign of victory. We stood together, staring at the ragged hole in the door, silently making our own individual plans for survival for the devastation that would accompany our parents' return. Reasons, excuses, and full-blown lies careened around in my head as I tried in vain to come up with a viable explanation.

Turns out there was no viable explanation, and Rowdy and I were forced to give up not only our obligatory sparklers, but fully fifty percent of our Black Cat supply. We also lost our bow privileges for approximately a year and had hard labor for six months to pay off the new door. Larry, on the other hand, got nothing. He was not required to give up even a single sparkler for his abhorrent behavior. I've long held that against him, and even to this day I have in my possession an M-80 with his name on it.

Now that I'm a grown man, with kids of my own, I can readily see what my own parents must have gone through around the fourth. I've tried to emphasize to my kids the importance of being responsible with fireworks. We have spent many quality hours blowing stuff up, but always in the safest manner. I have shared my knowledge of the old "can in the water" trick, the firecracker rocket, and, of course, everyone's favorite, the firecracker in the can surrounded by water *and* dipped in gasoline. It is sad, however, that my kids had no neighbors growing up who were willing to exchange loaded arrows with them. For most of their young lives, our neighbors were old people whom had long since lost their sense of adventure where explosive devises were concerned. For fear of causing a heart attack, or even possibly running an arrow clear through an aged body, the kids were precluded from this wonderful activity.

My son, Kellen, has turned out to be a sort of explosive prodigy. His love for the Fourth of July is very similar to mine. It is not uncommon for him to be missing a fingernail or two in the month of July, just like his old dad. It seems his own creativity in the manipulation of fireworks even surpasses mine as he grows older. He was, after all, the one who introduced me to the world of "sparkler bombs." These formidable units are fashioned out of wire sparklers, and a significant amount of duct tape, and have roughly the explosive power of the old M-80s. The first time I saw and heard one of these things, I couldn't believe it. It was truly a magnificent explosion, and it made me long for all those sparklers my parents had confiscated all those years ago. I wonder if they still have them.

Chapter 23
A HARROWING EXPERIENCE

I would like to take a pause in this book and give some mention to my little brother, Ronald James.

I've written about Ron in some of my other stories. Usually his name comes up with some derogatory comment attached. There is a logical explanation for that, and it is simply that for most of my developing years, from '68 to '80, Ron was a near constant source of aggravation to me. Frankly, I didn't like him very much. That's not to say I hated him or didn't love him as a brother, as I can honestly say I put a kid in the hospital defending his honor. It's just that I always saw Ron as a pampered, conniving, doted-over little menace, sent from hell to destroy my heretofore perfect life.

From the time Ron could string sentences together, I would be willing to bet that the twenty-four-hour periods that passed without us bickering at some point could be counted on one hand.

One of those days, however, took placc in the aftermath of one of my most vivid childhood memories.

It was summer in the year of our bicentennial, 1976. I had just turned fourteen and was scheduled to start high school in the fall. I was awakened one morning, like many, many others, by my mother's stirring rendition of *"Oh, What a Beautiful Morning."* I always preferred that wake up song to Mom's other favorite, "IT'S TIME TO GET UP! IT'S TIME TO GET UP!" The hip hip hooray of that song always shot any chance I might have had of having a "beautiful morning," I can assure you.

On this day I remembered that I got to harrow the pasture. I say *got* to, instead of *had* to, because that was a job I truly enjoyed. It involved driving and, tractor or not, at age fourteen any steering wheel would do nicely. It was a job that also could easily be made to last all day, thus avoiding the possibilities of other less-stimulating chores that my mom never seemed to run short of.

Driving the tractor round and round the field over a period of hours, I found, was very conducive to daydreaming, my favorite pastime. The droning of the engine and the endless clanking of the harrow as it bounced along behind worked as a sort of hypnotist pendulum, and one's imagination could run rampant. Instead of harrowing a field, I could be running the Indy 500, driving, announcing, and doing color commentary all at the same time—and I usually was.

And so it was that day. I had been running hard that morning, and I had a pretty sizable lead over A.J. Foyt and Richard Petty in the big 2K Ranch 500. So sizable, in fact, that I decided I could afford a pit, meaning unhook the harrow and drive my race car (tractor) up to the house for a bite of lunch.

I walked into the house, plopped down in a chair at the kitchen table, and let out a long, loud sigh to signify to Mom that I had been slaving my tail off all morning, and if I didn't get something to eat, and soon, I'd probably pass out. Much to my delight, Mom heard me roaring up the hill from the pasture and presented me with a gourmet Spam sandwich. Nothing like monkey meat to a starving race car (tractor) driver. As I sat, munching away at my sandwich and staring out our large picture window at the racecourse (field) I'd been driving on, I tried to mentally calculate just how many laps remained.

Since I had always been bad at math, I was deep in thought when Ron walked in and sat down in the chair next to me. He said "hello" or "hi," or something like that, bringing me out of my math-induced coma. On a normal day, I would have seen his actions as a sneak attack and a deliberate attempt to botch my mental math and would set into motion appropriate counter measures, like a swift backhand or a verbal barrage worthy of his insolence. This day, however, I was able to shake the urge for retaliation and simply grunted my recognition. Ron—quite perceptive for an eight year old and seeing that I was in one of my better moods—set about an onslaught of chatter as only he could. I chose to go along with it, grunting at what I deemed to be the correct pauses in his endless prattle, as my mind drifted back to the race after lunch.

When I had finished eating, Ron, who was still jabbering, saw that his semi-attentive audience was fixing to leave and popped up a bold request.

"Can I go with ya?" he asked, using his best "puppy dog eyes" routine.

Since I had long been immune to those droopy eyes, I hastily said, "NO WAY!" and glanced to Mom for confirmation. I got none, as usual, and I began reeling off reasons why Ron shouldn't go. He was too young, he'd have to stand for hours, he talked too much, et cetera, et cetera. Mom, who I'm sure had been exposed to Ron's incessant chatter all morning, saw a chance for a little peace and quiet and turned on me with *her* best "puppy dog" look.

"Couldn't you take him for just an hour or so? He really loves to go and needs to learn how to drive the tractor, and you're the best harrower I've got."

She was ruthless. The eyes that I regrettably hadn't developed immunity to, coupled with a blatant self-esteem boost—what could I say?

"Okay, but just for an hour, then he *walks* up to the house," I mumbled.

As Ron and I walked out to the tractor, I thought about what Mom had said. Something like, "You're the best tractor driver in the world." I smiled at her grasp of the obvious.

Anyone who didn't happen to grow up on a farm may not realize it, but a tractor only has one seat. Therefore, a passenger on such a vehicle is required to stand on the foot railing and hold on to the fender of the rear wheel to try to steady himself. This was the position Ron took as I brought the tractor to life. As I started it, I tried to explain as simply as I could the finer points of driving a tractor to Ron. I'm not sure how much he retained, as the engine was quite loud, but I demonstrated how to lift the bucket on the front and the counter balance on the rear. I then went on to explain that our particular tractor was equipped with a Selecto-Speed Transmission, and it actually had ten forward gears.

Ron didn't seem overly impressed with my knowledge of the inner workings of the vehicle and was impatient to get moving. I deftly slipped the tranny into third, and down the hill we went. All the way down the hill, my mother's words kept popping into my mind. "You're the most awesome tractor driver in the known universe."

"Yes," I thought to myself, "there is surely no greater tractor driver than I, and it's high time Ron sees just how lucky he is to have me for a big brother."

When we hit the bottom of the hill and the road that crossed the field, I looked over at Ron, who had a death grip on the fender as we bounced along.

"Hang on, bud!" I shouted over the roar of the engine. "We're gonna see how fast this baby'll go."

I slid the transmission to number ten and pulled open the throttle. Ron, who didn't have enough sense to be afraid, grinned from ear to ear as the tractor lurched forward, gaining speed with every foot we covered. Since tractors aren't equipped with speedometers, I really don't have any idea how fast we were going after about three hundred yards. I can say it became too darn fast in a hurry.

As we raced along at warp speed, we began to run into some turbulence—namely bumps in the road—and it only took one time of our wheels coming completely off the ground for me to realize it was time to slow down. Again I shouted at Ron to hang on and grabbed for the throttle control lever. I shut the throttle down, but our momentum carried us along at a tremendous rate, and I was beginning to worry as the bumps continued to send us airborne. I made a grab for the gearshift as Ron, still grinning widely, clung to the fender. My plan was to shift down a couple gears at a time, thus allowing the compression to slow us down. Unfortunately, we hit another bump as my hand closed upon the shift knob, jolting the tractor and causing me to go from tenth to third gear. The engine screamed as our wheels made contact with the ground, and I was jerked forward toward the steering wheel.

Out of the corner of my eye I saw Ron, still smiling, be ripped from his perch beside me and plop down neatly on his back directly behind the front wheel of the still-speeding tractor. My first reaction was to stand on the brakes, hoping that by some miracle I could stop before the huge rear tire rolled over his small body. Apparently, it wasn't my day for miracles, for as soon as the brakes locked up, the tires began to slide.

It all must have happened in a matter of seconds, but I recall having an image of sliding over Ron and smearing him all over the field. I let my foot off the brake and watched as the rear tire bounced over Ron's midsection, knowing I had just killed my little brother. After I had cleared Ron, I again dynamited the brakes and the tractor finally slid to a halt.

Slowly, almost reluctantly, I turned my head, sure that I would see Ron's limp, lifeless body lying behind me. There was a shrill noise ringing in my ears as I turned and stepped from the now quiet machine. I soon determined what that shrill noise was as I saw Ron, up and presumably alive, sprinting toward the house, screaming like a banshee.

Now, I'm no doctor, but I know enough that you shouldn't move an injured person, and injured I was sure he was. I felt it my duty to run him down, tackle him, and hold him down till I could call an ambulance or perhaps a hearse.

I had no trouble overtaking him, as I was much older and faster, and with a nice flying leg sweep, he toppled safely to the ground. I tried in vain to convince him to stop kicking and flailing about so that I might have a look at his wounds and determine if he had a broken back or neck. I was able to determine by his volume that there was nothing wrong with his respiratory system and decided it would be safe for me to get off of him and let him up.

He was up like a shot, making a bee line for the house, screaming at the top of his lungs when my mother stepped out of house and hollered, "What the ----- is going on down there?!"

I found it extremely difficult to shout back to my mom that I had run over her baby with the tractor, so I sat down in the field and did what seemed the most natural thing to do. I cried. I knew that as soon as Ron topped the hill, which gauging by his speed would be about fifteen seconds, the truth would come pouring out, and I would be in more trouble than I could possibly imagine.

I saw Ron top the hill and run to Mom's arms. I saw her scoop him up and run into the house, then back outside to the car and go speeding up the driveway. I was as low as I had ever been as I sat in that field crying and cursing my stupidity. I guess I'd sat there ten or fifteen minutes before my grandpa came driving down to the field and walked over to my side.

I can't remember much of what was said between us, other than the fact that my mother had called him before she took Ron to the hospital and asked him to come down and make sure I was all right. The fact that she even cared at that point was shocking, but a comfort, nonetheless.

As it turned out, Ron came through his ordeal relatively unscathed, except for a bruise in the shape of a tractor tread across his chest. I'm sure, thinking back, it was a small price to pay for the tremendous amount of leverage it gained him in the years to follow. Besides, how many people can tell their grandchildren that they were run over by the "GREATEST TRACTOR DRIVER IN THE GALAXY"?

Chapter 24

IT'S A CRASH TEST, DUMMY

Ever since I was a kid, I've had a love-hate relationship with motorcycles. I love them, and they, in turn, hate me.

It seems that since I bought my first bike, a well-used Honda Trail 50, it has been my role in the world of motorcyclists to be a sort of crash test dummy. Of course I have never received any compensation for this vital role, and I have only occasionally been asked to relay my findings to anyone but immediate family. However, without the knowledge that all of my motorcycle mishaps serve a vital role in the betterment of cycle research and development, the years of bumps, bruises, and broken bones would surely not have been worth it.

Some of my more memorable contributions came in the early seventies when motorcycle riding was seeing its first major boom period. At the time, I was living on a large cattle ranch some twenty-five miles north west of Bonners Ferry, Idaho. This is where I tested the limits of a Honda 50, as well as the body of an eight year old. Much of the testing involved suspension and the effect of not having any might have in relation to how many times an eight-year-old body could be tossed to the ground as a result of it.

I came to the following conclusions . . .

A Honda 50 should never be ridden at top speed, thirty-five miles per hour, on any surface that is not paved. Any deflection of the front end at this speed 99.9 percent of the time results in the immediate and violent abuse to the bike, not to mention the eight-year-old body astride of it. Also, a Honda 50 should never, under any circumstances, be ridden at top speed, thirty-five miles per hour, on any surface that is paved. On pavement, at this speed, on this particular motorcycle, one is sure to experience a condition known in the motorcycling community as "head shake" 99.9 percent of the time. This is where the front wheel begins to whip back and forth, quickly and violently, invariably sending the bike and its rider skidding along the smooth, but rather unforgiving, paved surface.

The one other thing I was able to determine through years of testing at the ranch was an extremely important one to anyone considering using a Honda 50 for the purpose of herding cattle. Now I urge each of you considering this application of your Honda 50 to read this very carefully. A Honda 50 should never, never be operated at top speed when trying to catch up to a stampeding herd of cattle, fresh off the pasture. The combination of cow excrement, speed, and the small wheels and wide tires of your cycle one hundred percent of the time spell disaster. Without fail, you are bound to find your eight-year-old body clinging to your prone motorcycle while being deluged by any and all remnants of said stampeding herd of cattle. I should note that cow excrement is extremely difficult to remove from one's riding gear, as well as the internal workings of your motorcycle.

As I grew older, I realized that I had completed every conceivable test of my Honda 50 and saw it was time to take on the bigger bikes. That being the Honda SL70. Some of the more important contributions I was able to come up with for this particular motorcycle in the relatively short time that I owned it are as follows . . .

The Honda SL70 taillight will not prevent one who is attempting a world record third gear wheelie from flipping over backward, or "looping out" as it is called by moto-aficionados. I did this test many, many times, as it was my belief that any part that required as much room as an SL70 taillight should indeed serve a more vital purpose than telling the guy behind you that your foot is on the brake. Sadly, this is not the case. I believe this finding had a large part in the eventual demise of the SL model of motorcycles.

Another drawback of the SL line was that of its exhaust pipe design.

Being outfitted from the factory with a "down pipe" design of exhaust, it was susceptible to dents and dings, but more importantly, it was a nasty burn hazard to its crash victims. For instance, one time as I was riding in the old gravel pit near our home when I felt the need, as I often did, to do a little crash testing. I lined up with the nearest twelve-foot embankment I could find and plummeted off the face of it. The bike performed well in its initial endo phase, its front end dropping rapidly despite my futile attempts to pull it up, and the rear end followed nicely by kicking slightly over vertical during the plunge. The problem arose as the dust cleared on the ground. Seems I found myself trapped under the still running cycle, face down in a semi-conscious state. This was always an unfortunate position to end up in, as the Honda SL70 weighed in at approximately four hundred pounds, whereas I, being eleven or twelve at the time, tilted the scales at an impressive seventy pounds. As I lay there weighing my options, and hoping my older brother would soon be along to debrief me on my findings, I came to the realization that my rear end was on fire. Seems the bike's flawed down pipe design had come to roost in a most undesirable locale. Realizing that I could not move, nor could I remain in this awkward and uncomfortable position, I did what any experienced crash dummy would do. I screamed and flailed about for what was probably five minutes, but seemed like five hours. Finally Rowdy showed up and, after recovering from a near-fatal laugh attack, was able to pull the rolling branding iron from my well-done posterior. I did feel a little bad for my dear brother, as he did experience some abdominal discomfort from his brush with death by laughter.

Shortly after that day, thankfully, I was able to blow up the old SL, and I was treated to the first "brand new" motorcycle I had ever owned. A shiny new Honda XR75. I named it Clyde. As I have probably mentioned before, everything our family owned had a name. Clyde was an engineering masterpiece. It was only the second year that Honda had stepped up with a full blown race model 75cc motorcycle, thus I was sure they were in dire need of a fair amount of crash testing, and I was willing, ready, and able to oblige. I outfitted Clyde with a "Bassani" exhaust system, which added approximately three horsepower and roughly three hundred decibels, and set about doing my part for Honda's R&D program. I was loud, proud, and a menace to the entire neighborhood. It was great.

I found out that the XR performed well in the loop out tests, as it had no taillight to smash to bits, leaving litter on the roadway, not to mention embedded in the backside of its twelve-year-old rider. I did find that due to far superior suspension, the XR resisted endoing and also performed very well in the high-speed paved road test. Full speed checked out at a remarkable fifty-six miles per hour, which I found to be more than adequate for high-speed carnage. I did find an area where the XR came up a little short, however, and it is my hope that Honda heeded my bulletin on this shortcoming.

One day as my brother raced down a gravel road in the backwoods of North Idaho, I came around a corner in full power slide position and was faced with a narrow, single lane bridge. Now at fifty-six miles per hour, on gravel, in power slide position, when faced with an obstacle such as this, one does not have much time to react. My first inclination was, of course, to check for oncoming traffic. Thankfully, there was none. My next priority was to actually hit the bridge provided as a means of clearing the river some thirty feet below. I was able to accomplish this by regrettably letting off the throttle by the slightest amount possible. What I could not have factored in, however, was my bike's overwhelming desire to ride the two-by-twelve planks provided for car tires on the deck of the old bridge. Personally, I would have been more than happy to cross the bridge, neatly tucked between the planks, but Clyde, being a perfectionist to the bitter end, was having none of that notion. As the sides of my tires touched the planks, I was instantly thrown to the deck and began a fifty-five mile per hour combination slide/roll along the bridge's extremely rough and weathered surface. When I could look up between rolls, I could see Clyde skidding across the surface of the bridge also. Then, to my horror, I saw his tires catch, and he was launched into the air, flying toward the bridge's edge. Fortunately, he bounced off the guardrail provided for just such an emergency and tumbled back to the bridge's deck, rather than into the river below. Eventually I was able to stop my roll/slide, and it was immediately evident to me the drawback to crashing on an old wooden bridge. I greatly resembled a North American porcupine, as slivers up to twelve inches long protruded from every inch of my body. Believe me, I had stickers in places where heretofore I had no idea I even had places. Tattered, torn, and disheartened at this painful turn of events, I got to my feet, shook the cobwebs out of my rattled brain, and surveyed my situation. Plucking slivers, I limped toward my upended mount as my brother, whose cackles could be heard over the roar of his own cycle, came riding up to join me as I hefted my fallen comrade back onto his wheels. It was at this point that I realized a particularly nasty sliver had penetrated the top of my old canvas tennis shoe and had pinned my pinky toe to the bottom of said shoe. This realization created a combination of horror and hilarity, depending on your perspective, mine or my sadistic brother's. After several attempts, and a good deal of laughter accompanied by equal amounts of tears and cursing, again depending on who you happened to be, my pinky was saved and we were once again ready to resume further testing. Clyde, for his part, performed outstandingly. For other than a couple of torn grips and a sliver or two imbedded in his seat cover, he came out of the mishap unscathed. In my report to Honda, I related my findings of the XR's tendency to make poor judgments at high speeds on wooden single lane bridges. I never heard back, so I assumed they had alleviated this problem by the next year's production.

As time passed, my desire to serve as loyal R&D dummy for the motorcycle industry waned, and by my mid-teens, I found myself bike-less. It was at that point that I tried my hand at another mode of crash testing, which involved four wheels, rather than two. But that is an entirely different story for another time.

Chapter 25

HI HO SILVER!

It was a clear, sunny day that July in 1974, and Rowdy and I were looking forward to yet another day of motorcycle riding near our home in Colbert, Washington. Little did we know that this would end up being a day we would never forget.

My dad, who had been away working all week in Sunnyside, Washington, joined us at the breakfast table.

"What do you boys have planned for today?" he asked as he poured a cup of steaming hot coffee.

"We're gonna do a little riding," I responded before chomping on another spoonful of Cocoa Puffs.

"How was the riding down in Sunnyside?" Rowdy asked, wiping the milk trail off his chin.

"It was great!" Dad said, and then he proceeded to tell us about his exploits riding with some friends of his after work.

Dad had a 1972 Honda XL250, which he had aptly named Silver. I say aptly because that is what color it was and, of course, my dad was always a huge Lone Ranger fan. It was also common practice in my family to name everything we ever owned.

Dad went on to tell us about this hill they had found that was unclimbable. Seems everyone had tried it, but to no avail. It was just too steep. As I listened, I found myself a little disbelieving and, as usual, felt compelled to express my doubts.

"There isn't a hill that can't be climbed," I stated matter-of-factly. "In fact," I went on, "I'll bet Rowdy or I could top it first try."

I glanced over at Rowdy for some back up, but he just stuffed another spoonful of cereal into his mouth and slowly shook his head.

Dad, who was content to let my apparent ego outbreak slide, simply smiled and said, "Well, Son, that may be."

It was a harmless enough comment, but somehow it smacked of doubt in my twelve-year-old ears. Doubt was not something I dealt with very well, and I felt compelled to try to persuade my father that what I'd said was not mere braggadocio, but pure, proven, unequivocal fact. After all, we climbed hills for a living! Every day, morning till night, we practically lived at the gravel pit a mile or so from our house. Gravel, sand, dirt—you name it—we climbed, jumped, or sidehilled it. So, to me, it only stood to reason that simply because a hill was in a different geographical location, there was no reason for it to be insurmountable. It was simply a matter of technique.

Dad listened patiently as I rattled on about what they should do: gears to be in, amount of run, keeping weight to the rear tire, et cetera, et cetera, until finally I guess his ears got tired or he could simply take no more of my prattle. He held up his hand for me to stop.

"Maybe," he said, "you guys should just take me on over to the pit and show me how the pros do it."

Now, this took me completely off guard.

"You want to go to the pit with us?" I asked in astonishment.

"Sure," he said, "looks like a nice day for it."

"Yahoo!" I blurted. "Looks like Christmas in July!"

You see my dad was a very busy man. When he wasn't working to put food on the table, or gas in our motorcycles, he was remodeling the house, fixing our motorcycles, or some other item on the ever-present honey-do list. So, his chances to go riding with us were few and far between. I jumped up from the table, completely disregarding my remaining Cocoa Puffs, and shot back to my room to get ready.

As Rowdy and I were gassing up our bikes, we talked about which hills we should take Dad on, each of us speculating on his abilities and those of his bike.

"He can make any of them, really," Rowdy said. "Silver has lots of power and a good tire. So, as long as he can stay on, he should be able to climb anything."

"Even the Widow Maker?" I asked skeptically.

"Like I said, *if* he can stay on," Rowdy chuckled.

I chuckled, too, somewhat nervously, as I considered the thought of Dad challenging the mother of all hills. The Widow Maker was a long, very steep hill, which consisted of mostly loose gravel, but with a fairly hard base. The last three or four feet of this particular hill posed its greatest challenge. At this point, one was faced with a fairly large "belly," or an area from which the soil has eroded or sloughed away, leaving an overhang slightly more than vertical. Usually on hills such as this, there is one line or groove that a rider must hit in order to get over the top and avoid flipping over backward and tumbling down the hill.

Before we left the yard, I asked Dad what kind of hills he felt up to climbing.

"I'll go wherever you go," he said. And we were off.

When we arrived at the pit, we did our usual safety lap, zipping around the huge gravel piles to make sure that no one had gouged out any areas with a loader, leaving deadly drop-offs where there had been none before. Seeing there were none, we began climbing the various gravel piles in the upper pit area. Up and down, round and round, we went for probably an hour, all the while keeping an eye on Dad to try to get a read on his talents. I have to say he'd come a long way since the last time we'd seen him ride. In fact, it seemed he was even starting to look somewhat natural on ol' Silver. Since for most of our lives the only thing Rowdy and I had seen him astride was a horse, for a while he looked a little goofy aboard a motorcycle. This day, however, we were seeing a different side.

"You think he's ready for the lower pit?" Rowdy asked as we sat atop a hill, letting our bikes cool and watching Dad climb an adjacent hill.

"He's doing pretty good," I said as I watched him come down the hill and head in our direction.

When Dad pulled up beside us and shut down his engine, he grinned and asked, "Is this as tough as it gets around here?"

Rowdy and I snorted in unison.

"Hardly. You ready for the lower pit?" Rowdy asked, glancing in my direction. My reaction was mixed. On the one hand I was ready to go to the bottom pit, and Dad seemed to be bent on challenging his limits. But on the other hand, I just wasn't sure he was ready for what lay below.

"Sure!" Dad replied. "Let's look at some tough stuff. What about that Widow Maker you boys are always talking about? I think I'd like to give that a go."

My heart practically jumped out of my mouth.

As we started our bikes and wound our way to the bottom

pit, I couldn't stop hoping that once Dad got a look at the Widow Maker his good sense would take over and I wouldn't have to be a witness to his untimely demise. I was soon to find out, however, that I'd grossly overestimated his good sense.

When we reached the flat in the bottom, we pulled up side by side and shut off our engines, surveying what lay before us. I had climbed the Widow Maker many times, but somehow on this day it looked particularly ominous.

"Well, there she is," Rowdy said, reaching his arms out ahead of him and opening them with a flourish.

"You guys climb that?" Dad asked, as if this was all some horrific joke.

"All the time!" I piped up, suddenly feeling awash in pride at Dad's obvious disbelief.

"What gear?" Dad asked, obviously considering trying it.

"I try to hit the bottom in fourth, then hit third half way up," Rowdy explained. "Robb gets fifth and shifts twice," he went on.

I could hardly believe my ears. Surely, I thought, Rowdy can see that he is encouraging his own father to commit suicide. He was not ready for this; I was sure of it. He could be killed, maimed, or even worse—he could completely ruin a perfectly good motorcycle!

"Are you really thinking about going up?" I had to ask.

"Sure," he replied. "Any advice from the pros?"

Instantly, I realized what had become of Dad's good sense. This was a matter of *principle*. Obviously, I had talked too much this morning and had inadvertently thrown out a gauntlet. This realization also made me sure beyond a shadow of a doubt that Dad would indeed try the Widow Maker. All I could do was offer whatever advice I could muster.

"Okay," I started, "get a good run. I'd start from about that weed patch," I said, pointing to a patch of knapweed about twenty yards behind where we were sitting. "Wrap it up and try to get fourth gear before the bottom. About half way up it gets kinda loose, so keep your weight back so you don't start spinning. If you start to lug, you may have to shift down. Be quick. If you are too slow, you'll lose your momentum, and you won't make it."

"The most important thing, though," I continued, "is if you make it to the belly, you have got to let off the gas. You'll still make it, but you have got to get off the gas." As I said this, I looked into his eyes to make sure he understood the significance of what I'd just told him.

"Got it?" I asked.

"Got it," he replied. "Start there, fourth gear, and wrap it," he said, smiling with satisfaction.

"And what else?" I asked, feeling much more like a parent than I was ready for.

"Oh yeah," he laughed. "Let off the gas at the belly."

I shook my head in disbelief that he truly didn't realize the seriousness of the situation.

"We'll go first so you can kinda see what he is talking about," Rowdy said as he started his bike and headed back to the starting point.

He sat for a few seconds, revving his engine. Varoom, boom, boom, boom. Then he dropped the clutch and was off like a shot. He smoothly grabbed gears, sending gravel spewing out behind him. At the halfway point, you could see he'd shifted down to third only by the slightest fish tail of his rear tire. Onward and upward he went, till finally he bounced smoothly over the belly and topped the hill.

"You see how he let off at the top?" I shouted to Dad over the roar of my now running cycle. He nodded and smiled with a look that assured me he hadn't understood a word I'd said.

My trip up the hill was much the same as Rowdy's, except

for the fact that I had to shift twice to muster enough power from my little Honda XR75 to make it over the top. I always felt that made my climbs more difficult. That, however, was always a matter of some contention with big brother.

When I reached the top, I could hardly get my bike shut off quickly enough as I hurried to the edge to join Rowdy in watching the drama that was about to unfold.

Dad started Silver and rolled back to the weed patch I'd pointed out. We could hear him revving his engine, probably contemplating his mortality and quite possibly his principles.

Gravel shot from behind him as he let go of the clutch and cracked the throttle. My heart beat wildly as Rowdy began doing his own personal play by play.

"And he's off!" he shouted, sounding every bit the horse race caller.

"He's got second gear. There's third, and now fourth," Rowdy continued.

"Oh my gosh. Oh my gosh," I mumbled to myself.

"He's at the bottom of the hill, screamin' like a turpentine cat!" Rowdy shouted, keeping to his call.

"Oh my gosh. Oh my gosh," I said louder now, as I could now make out the look on Dad's face.

"He's at the halfway point folks, and by golly he's flyin'!" Rowdy went on.

"Oh my gosh! Oh my gosh!" I was now shouting because I could see Dad's eyes, the size of dinner plates, and gauged his speed at approximately 120 miles per hour.

"He's not going to let off!" I screamed desperately to Rowdy.

"He's still picking up speed at the three quarter mark. Warp speed. Beam him up, Scotty!" Rowdy's call had, at this point, become just slightly out of control.

"Oh my gosh! Oh my gosh!" I shouted over and over as I

saw Dad reaching the base of the belly. He *was not* letting off. "Hi Ho Silver, away!" Rowdy shouted as Dad and Silver shot over the hill at approximately mach one.

"Oh my gosh! Oh . . . My . . . Gosh!"

Dad and his bike shot straight up, probably twenty feet. Then, at the apex of their flight, the bike slowly nosed down like a disabled fighter plane. Down, down they plummeted, nose first.

Rowdy and I stood silently, mouths agape, knowing the end was near, and all that was left was to scrape up the carnage. We didn't have to wait long.

Dad's front wheel made first contact with the ground, followed almost immediately by the top of his head. He carried out a near perfect headstand. That was until Silver continued his own somersault, slamming Dad to the ground before him.

When the dust cleared, Dad resembled Wyle E. Coyote, of Road Runner fame, as he was neatly imbedded in the gravel and dust. Rowdy and I just stood there, staring at the wreckage that lay before us, hoping for signs of life. We both knew what had to be done. First and foremost, we slowly walked over and gently lifted Silver back to his wheels. Eventually, Dad began to stir, and after a time, he was able to get himself into a quasi-upright position. He spit dirt and gravel for—oh, I don't know—two to three hours, till finally he had excavated enough to be able to make words.

"Wow, what a ride. Guess I should have let off at the top, huh?" he said, smiling at me with grit-filled teeth.

"Well," I said, "that's the way the pros do it."

Chapter 26

GATES OF HELL

All eyes in Mr. Gates' seventh grade class at Mead Middle School focused on me as I sweated bullets and contemplated the answer I was about to give.

It was 1974. I was twelve years old. I remember that because the World's Fair was about to take place a mere fifteen miles from where my family lived at the time.

Our family had undergone many changes, most of which centered on my father's occupation. We had left the ranch and our home in Bonners Ferry, Idaho, to seek fortune and fulfillment in the larger world.

Dad took a job with a company called All West Breeders, which was, as the name would indicate, an artificial insemination service, based out of Mt. Vernon, Washington.

The process of artificial insemination was still relatively new at that time, and there weren't that many people qualified to do it. Therefore, my father, as a technician, was in high demand with the dairies in the area, and he thoroughly loved his job. Personally, I found the process somewhat revolting and even undignified.

The farmers all loved it because they were no longer forced to keep a bull on the premises, which saved them hay, pasture, and being forced to watch a non-milk-producing herd member swagger around in their fields, manufacturing nothing but testosterone and fertilizer—that and the fact that dairy bulls have a tendency to be very ill-tempered and often won't let the farmers walk through their own fields. These factors combined to make artificial insemination a very attractive option to the farmers. I'm not sure that the bull population was all that thrilled by it.

We were all very happy for Dad, but, alas, I found myself having far more difficulty adjusting to my new surroundings than he did. I was finding school extremely difficult, and it just seemed I didn't fit in. I was a country mouse gone city, and I'm afraid it must have shown. My feet, having been shaped at birth to cowboy boots, were having a tough time adjusting to tennis shoes, and for the first time in my life, I felt just plain awkward. Even when playing sports, which I had always done pretty well in, I felt clumsy and inadequate. Part of that feeling I'm sure was caused by the fact that here there were fifty talented kids in my grade, where before there had been five. The other part was probably that at age twelve, I *was* pretty awkward.

Entering seventh grade, I had a year of middle school experience under my belt, and things were actually starting to come around for me. I had some friends that I'd made the year before, my feet were finally adjusting, and slowly, ever so slowly, I was beginning to fit in with all the city mice.

All was flowing pretty smoothly in my little river of life until one fateful day in Mr. Gates' social studies class. By the time that class was completed, my little river had become a raging torrent, complete with a nice little ninety-foot waterfall that emptied into a pool of despair.

Class started out pretty simply that day, as it was a Friday. Therefore, Mr. Gates, normally a very stern man, was in remarkably good humor. So much so, in fact, that at one point in science class he told a funny story about blowing up some lab in college. Since we all enjoyed explosions, the entire class applauded his efforts.

After he had quieted us down and instructed us to get out our social studies books, he paused and said, "No, instead get out a sheet of paper. We're going to do something a little different today."

Now the word "different" has always been a word that sets off bells of warning in my brain, and this was no exception. "Pop quiz," I muttered to myself. "How could he? He was in such a good mood, too." I pulled out my paper and prepared myself for the inevitable barrage of questions that I was sure I had no answers for.

"Today," he said, "we're going to look into what makes our society tick."

He went on to explain about government, business, and the private sector and how they work and affect our lives. "I'm interested to know a little bit about each of your families and where they fit into our society," Mr. Gates said. "What I want to do is go around the class and have each of you tell us if you live in a house or an apartment, how many people are in your family, and what your parents do for a living," he instructed.

My first reaction was one of relief. I knew the answers to these questions and thought to myself that it might be interesting to see how all of these city dwellers lived. I sat back and mulled the questions over in my mind, as well as the answers I might give.

"Let's see," I thought. "I live in a house, a nice house I

might say. There are five people in my family. Mom works at home...." I thought I should say that, as I didn't want anyone thinking she just lazed around the house watching soap operas all day. "And Dad, of course, was a ..." My stomach did a double twisting back flip, lodging itself firmly in my throat. No one had ever asked me what my dad did for a living before, and the thought of explaining the process of artificial insemination to an entire class of seventh graders made my head spin. I couldn't believe this was happening, just when I had clawed my way up to being only the fifth biggest dork in the seventh grade.

I made a quick mental count of the kids I thought would go before me and glanced at the clock. I tried to calculate how many minutes each kid would talk, added that together with any comments Mr. Gates may have, and divided that by total class time remaining and came up with a total of ... trouble.

The answers were coming very quickly, as the students all seemed to enjoy the opportunity to brag about their stuff and parents. Soon there were only three students left before I would be asked to answer. My mind raced as I struggled with what I would say. "Maybe," I thought to myself, "if I said it fast enough no one would hear what I said, or I could just use the initials A.I. Maybe I should just say we are on Welfare. Maybe ..." it was my turn. I shifted nervously in my seat as all eyes turned to me.

"There are five people in my family. We live in a nice house in the country. My mom works at home, and my dad breeds cows."

The words crashed like cymbals in my ears even as they rolled off my tongue. Why had I said THAT?! My dad *breeds cows*, just as plain as that. I sat in shocked silence, as did the rest of the class. There was not a sound except for those four words banging around the obviously empty confines of my head.

After what seemed like a couple hours, Mr. Gates broke the deafening silence.

"Well," Mr. Gates drawled, serious as a preacher, "he must be very tired when he gets home."

The class erupted like a giant laughter volcano, and my life, it seemed, was over.

I think Mr. Gates realized that his comment had been perhaps slightly inappropriate for a science teacher, and he tried to regain order in the classroom. He promptly chastised the most vocal joke hurlers and whacked his ever-present yardstick across his desk. That brought most of the class back to attention, except me, of course, as it is hard to come from a puddle under one's desk to attention.

Mr. Gates went on to explain about artificial insemination and its growingly important role in the farming community. He then apologized for his comment and said that I should indeed be proud of what my father did. But I didn't hear a word. Instead, I kept going over and over what kind of picture had popped into everyone's minds when I had been possessed to blurt out the words I had. There were a million things I could have said, but for some reason unbeknownst to me, I hadn't, and the reason eludes me to this day.

Mine, it turned out, was the final presentation of the day, and thankfully the bell rang, signaling the end of school for the week. I sat at my desk as the rest of the students filed out, hoping that by some miracle they would all be abducted by terrorists over that weekend or perhaps be afflicted with some rare form of amnesia.

Oddly enough, there may have been a bit of amnesia going around that weekend, as aside from a few derogatory "moos" that following Monday morning, I heard very little about the whole incident. It seemed I still maintained my distinction of being only the fifth biggest dork in my class.

Over that weekend I made a decision about what my career path would be. I would be a fireman, a policeman, or even a doctor or janitor, but I was sure I would never choose a profession that would cause my children grief if they were asked to answer the same question I was on that day.

I'm proud to say that I'm in the rubber business—err, tires, that is.

ABOUT THE AUTHOR

Robb MacDonald was born in 1962 in a small town in North Idaho, called Bonners Ferry. Born the second son of a rodeo cowboy, his formative years were dominated by two major influences, horses and his older sibling, Rowdy.

Currently he resides in Libby, Montana, with his lovely wife, Jeannie. Robb has two grown children, a daughter, Aubree, and son, Kellen, who both live in the same town with their children, Landyn, Cylus, Paislee Mae, and Weslee. A very special daughter-in-law, Casie, rounds out the close-knit group, which gives meaning to life in the present.

The proprietor of a retail tire outlet in Libby, Robb's writing is done on a "catch as catch can" basis, and the stories that make up this book were compiled over a period of some fifteen years and a lifetime of memories.

PHOTOGRAPHY

A special thanks to the family of the late Edgar Stephenson of Valley Studios for their gracious permission to use the majority of the images found in this book.

Also to my niece, Mica Jae Johnson, of MicaJae's Photography, who put considerable time and effort into scanning, reformatting, and generally doing what was necessary to get these photos ready for print.